CW01080949

Jelly Recipe Book
Delicious Artisan Homemade Jelly Recipes for the Whole Family

Sun in Jars

Book 1

Brendan Fawn

Introduction

When we talk about jellies we always imagine something sweet, pleasant and fragrant. For me, jellies are associated with the summer and sun. When I hear the word jelly, I see colorful pictures of summer and a lot of sun.

Jellies could be prepared from any fruits or berries - both traditional as apples, strawberries, raspberries, gooseberries or pears, and exotic ones, for example, mango, pineapple, bananas or papaya. Some fans of unusual sweet desserts prepare jellies from carrots, tomatoes, cucumbers, oranges, or nuts.

Jellies can have different forms, colors, and tastes and can be liquid or thick, sour, very sweet or with a hint of sweetness or sourness. We can cook them with the sugar, honey, stevia or syrup (maple syrup). Jellies have orange, red, purple, pink, dark blue and many other colors.

In this cookbook, you will find traditional, homemade strawberry, raspberry, gooseberry jellies, but also few exotic ones with the pineapple, oranges or tangerines. Everyone will find tasty jellies for himself.

Jellies – Sunny Harvest

Summer is the time when we can enjoy sweet and colorful fruits, but what about winter? How to preserve those sunny days and sweet tastes? People invented jellies. Delicious and fragrant jelly, with the taste and smell of the sun and heat, is especially pleasant to taste during the cold winter period, recalling the hot and sunny summer. Moreover, family tea is hard to imagine without the fragrant and sweet raspberry or blackcurrant jelly, which is loved by both children and adults. Tea with a tempting sweet jelly dessert brings people together, provides an opportunity to socialize, communicate and enjoy delicious fruit desserts.

Jellies are preserving the taste of natural berries and fruits, but what is more, sweet fruit desserts improve mood and give a piece of summer and summer heat. Fruit jellies also fill us with energy and vitality and are healthy, because they contain various vitamins, minerals, and trace elements.

Each housewife has her own secrets of how to prepare delicious redcurrant, blackcurrant, strawberry, raspberry, apple, pear, quince, gooseberry, sweet cherry or apricot jelly.

There are many ways to process the fruits to cook delicious jellies, among which everyone can choose the right one. However, there are general cooking rules and some subtleties that every housewife should know.

In this cookbook, you will find how to prepare classic and tasty homemade jellies. Enjoy!

Blackcurrant-Lemon Jelly

Prep Time: 1 hour│Makes: 8 10 oz jars

Ingredients:

3 lb blackcurrants

4 lemons, peeled and diced

2 tbsp. gelatin

4 cups of sugar

4 tbsp. lemon juice

How to Prepare:

1. Spoon 1 cup of the sugar over the berries and lemons.

2. Boil the blackcurrants and lemons over the low heat for around 30 minutes, stirring all the time. Pour in some water. Then mash the berries using the potato masher and strain the mixture to get 4-5 cups of juice.

3. In a saucepan, combine the juice with the remaining sugar and lemon juice. Spoon the gelatin and boil the juice for 30 minutes until thickened. The jelly should be thick enough to pour it into the jars. Skim the foam from the surface.

4. Remove the saucepan from the heat and pour the freshly cooked jelly into the sterilized jars.

5. Turn the jars upside down or boil for around 10 minutes and then leave to cool. Check the lids by pressing them with the finger. In case some of the jars with the jelly are unsealed, place them into the fridge or reprocess the unsealed jars.

Nutritional Information (1 tbsp):

Calories: 52; Total fat: 5 oz; Total carbohydrates: 9 oz; Protein: 4 oz

Rose Petal & Gooseberry Jelly

Prep Time: 50 min. | Makes: 6-7 11 oz jars

Ingredients:

45 oz gooseberries, fresh

5 oz fresh rose petals

5 cups of sugar

2 tbsp. pure vanilla extract

1 tbsp. citric acid or lemon juice

How to Prepare:

1. Spoon 4 tbsp. sugar over the gooseberries and set aside for few hours. Then mash the berries using the potato masher.

2. In a pan, heat the water and boil the rose petals on a low heat for about 15 minutes.

3. Pour some water and boil the berries over the low heat for around 15-20 minutes, stirring all the time. Then strain the gooseberries to get 4 cups juice.

4. In a saucepan, combine the juice with the sugar and rose petals. Boil the juice for 30 minutes. The jelly should be thick enough to pour it into the jars. Add the vanilla and citric acid.

5. Remove the saucepan from the heat and ladle the freshly cooked jelly into the sterilized jars and seal the jars.

6. Flip the jars upside down or boil for around 10 minutes and then leave to cool. Check the lids by pressing them with the finger. In case some of the jars with the rose petal jelly are unsealed, place them into the fridge or reprocess the unsealed jars.

Nutritional Information (1 tbsp):

Calories: 55; Total fat: 4 oz; Total carbohydrates: 10 oz; Protein: 4 oz

Cherry-Redcurrant Jelly

Prep Time: 50 min.⎪Makes: 6-7 11 oz jars

Ingredients:

6 cups of redcurrants, fresh

2 cups of sweet cherry syrup

5 cups of sugar

1 tbsp. pure vanilla extract

How to Prepare:

1. Spoon 4 tbsp. sugar over the redcurrants and set aside for few hours and then mash the berries with the potato masher.

2. Pour some water and boil the redcurrants over the low heat for around 15-20 minutes, stirring all the time. Then strain the redcurrants to get 4 cups of the juice.

3. In a saucepan, combine the juice with the cherry syrup and sugar and boil the juice for 30 minutes. The jelly should be thick enough to ladle it into the jars. If not, add more sugar. Remove the foam from the surface.

4. Remove the saucepan from the heat and ladle the freshly cooked jelly into the sterilized jars and seal the jars.

5. Flip the jars upside down or boil for around 10 minutes and then leave to cool. Check the lids by pressing them with the finger. In case some of the jars with the redcurrant jelly are unsealed, place them into the fridge or reprocess the unsealed jars.

Nutritional Information (1 tbsp):

Calories: 54; Total fat: 2 oz; Total carbohydrates: 9 oz; Protein: 3 oz

Gooseberry Jelly

Prep Time: 50 min. | *Makes: 6-7 11 oz jars*

Ingredients:

4 lb gooseberries

5 cups of sugar

1 tbsp. pure vanilla extract

How to Prepare:

1. Spoon 4 tbsp. sugar over the gooseberries and set aside for few hours and then mash the berries using the potato masher.

2. Pour some water and boil the berries over the low heat for around 15-20 minutes, stirring all the time. Then strain the gooseberries to get 5 cups of juice.

3. In a saucepan, combine the juice with the remaining sugar. Boil the juice for 30 minutes. The jelly should be thick enough to pour it into the jars.

4. Remove the saucepan from the heat and pour the freshly cooked jelly into the sterilized jars and seal the jars.

5. Flip the jars upside down or boil for around 10 minutes and then leave to cool. Check the lids by pressing them with the finger. In case some of the jars with the gooseberry jelly are unsealed, place them into the fridge or reprocess the unsealed jars.

Nutritional Information (1 tbsp):

Calories: 59; Total fat: 4 oz; Total carbohydrates: 12 oz; Protein: 3.5 oz

Wild Cherry Jelly

Prep Time: 1 hour | Makes: 8-10 10 oz jars

Ingredients:

4 lbs wild cherries, pitted

5 cups of sugar

2 tsp. citric acid

How to Prepare:

1. Spoon 1 cup of sugar over the berries and set aside for overnight.

2. Pour some water and boil the berries over the low heat for around 30 minutes, stirring all the time. Then mash the berries with the potato masher and strain the mixture to get 4-5 cups of the juice.

3. In a saucepan, combine the juice with the remaining sugar and boil the juice for 30 minutes until thickened. The jelly should be thick enough to pour it into the jars. Skim the foam from the surface. 10 minutes before the jelly is ready mix in the citric acid.

4. Remove the saucepan from the heat and pour the freshly cooked jelly into the sterilized jars.

5. Turn the jars upside down or boil for around 10 minutes and then leave to cool. Check the lids by pressing them with the finger. In case some of the jars with the wild cherry jelly are unsealed, place them into the fridge or reprocess the unsealed jars.

Nutritional Information (1 tbsp):

Calories: 57; Total fat: 4 oz; Total carbohydrates: 8 oz; Protein: 3 oz

Apples & Orange Jelly

Prep Time: 1 hour | Makes: 8 10 oz jars

Ingredients:

2 lb apples, diced

4 oranges, peeled and diced

5 cups of sugar

2 tsp. cinnamon

How to Prepare:

1. Spoon 1 cup of the sugar over the apples and oranges. Set aside for overnight.

2. Boil the apples and oranges over the low heat for around 30 minutes, stirring all the time. Pour in some water. Then mash the apples and oranges using the potato masher and strain the mixture to get 4-5 cups of the juice.

3. In a saucepan, combine the juice with the remaining sugar and boil the juice for 30 minutes until thickened. The jelly should be thick enough to pour it into the jars. Skim the foam from the surface. 10 minutes before the jelly is ready mix in the cinnamon.

4. Remove the saucepan from the heat and pour the freshly cooked jelly into the sterilized jars.

5. Turn the jars upside down or boil for around 10 minutes and then leave to cool. Check the lids by pressing them with the finger. In case some of the jars with the jelly are unsealed, place them into the fridge or reprocess the unsealed jars.

Nutritional Information (1 tbsp):

Calories: 57; Total fat: 4 oz; Total carbohydrates: 8 oz; Protein: 3 oz

Rose Petals & Raspberries Jelly

Prep Time: 50 min.│ Makes: 6-7 11 oz jars

Ingredients:

25 oz raspberries, fresh

10 oz rose petals

5 cups of sugar

3 tbsp. pure vanilla extract

How to Prepare:

1. Spoon 4 tbsp. sugar over the raspberries. Set aside for few hours.

2. In a pan, heat the water and boil the rose petals on a low heat for about 15-20 minutes. Spoon some sugar.

3. Pour some water and boil the raspberries on a low heat for around 15-20 minutes, stirring all the time. Then strain the raspberries to get 4 cups of the juice.

4. In a saucepan, combine the juice with the sugar, rose petals and pure vanilla extract. Boil the juice for 30 minutes. The jelly should be thick enough to pour it into the jars.

5. Remove the saucepan from the heat and ladle the freshly cooked jelly into the sterilized jars and seal the jars.

6. Flip the jars upside down or boil for around 10 minutes and then leave to cool. Check the lids by pressing them with the finger. In case some of the jars with the rose petals raspberries jelly are unsealed, place them into the fridge or reprocess the unsealed jars.

Nutritional Information (1 tbsp):

Calories: 54; Total fat: 2 oz; Total carbohydrates: 9 oz; Protein: 3 oz

Cherry & Plum Jelly

Prep Time: 1 hour | *Makes: 6-7 11 oz jars*

Ingredients:

2 lbs cherries, pitted

1 lbs plums, pitted

5 cups of sugar

2 tsp. citric acid

How to Prepare:

1. Spoon 1 cup of sugar over the berries and set aside for overnight.

2. Pour some water and boil the berries over the low heat for around 30 minutes, stirring all the time. Then mash the berries with the potato masher and strain the mixture to get 4-5 cups of the juice.

3. In a saucepan, combine the juice with the remaining sugar and boil the juice for 30 minutes until thickened. The jelly should be thick enough to pour it into the jars. Skim the foam from the surface. 10 minutes before the jelly is ready mix in the citric acid.

4. Remove the saucepan from the heat and pour the freshly cooked jelly into the sterilized jars.

5. Turn the jars upside down or boil for around 10 minutes and then leave to cool. Check the lids by pressing them with the finger. In case some of the jars with the cherry jelly are unsealed, place them into the fridge or reprocess the unsealed jars.

Nutritional Information (1 tbsp):

Calories: 65; Total fat: 5 oz; Total carbohydrates: 7 oz; Protein: 3 oz

Raspberry Jelly

Prep Time: 50 min. | *Makes: 7-8 10 oz jars*

Ingredients:

25 oz raspberries, fresh

5 cups of sugar

1 medium lemon, halved and squeezed

3 tbsp. pure vanilla extract

How to Prepare:

1. Spoon 4 tbsp. sugar over the raspberries. Set aside for few hours. Then mash the raspberries using the potato masher.

2. Pour some water and boil the raspberries on a low heat for around 15-20 minutes, stirring all the time. Then strain the raspberries to get 4 cups of the juice.

3. In a saucepan, combine the juice with the sugar and pure vanilla extract. Pour the lemon juice. Boil the strawberry juice for 30 minutes. The jelly should be thick enough to pour it into the jars.

4. Remove the saucepan from the heat and ladle the freshly cooked jelly into the sterilized jars and seal the jars.

5. Flip the jars upside down or boil for around 10 minutes and then leave to cool. Check the lids by pressing them with the finger. In case some of the jars with the raspberry jelly are unsealed, place them into the fridge or reprocess the unsealed jars.

Nutritional Information (1 tbsp):

Calories: 52; Total fat: 3 oz; Total carbohydrates: 8 oz; Protein: 2 oz

Orange Taste Gooseberry Jelly

Prep Time: 50 min. | Makes: 6-7 11 oz jars

Ingredients:

4 lb gooseberries

1 orange, peeled and cubed

2 tbsp. orange zest, minced

1 tbsp. gelatin

5 cups of sugar

3 tbsp. pure vanilla extract

How to Prepare:

1. Spoon 4 tbsp. sugar over the gooseberries and set aside for few hours and then mash the fruits using the potato masher.

2. Pour some water and boil the gooseberries over the low heat for around 15-20 minutes, stirring all the time. Then strain the berries to get 4-5 cups of juice.

3. In a saucepan, combine the juice with the gooseberries, oranges, orange zest, pure vanilla extract, gelatin and the remaining sugar. Boil the juice for 30 minutes. The jelly should be thick enough to pour it into the jars.

4. Remove the saucepan from the heat and pour the freshly cooked jelly into the sterilized jars and seal the jars.

5. Flip the jars upside down or boil for around 10 minutes and then leave to cool. Check the lids by pressing them with the finger. In case some of the jars with the gooseberry jelly are unsealed, place them into the fridge or reprocess the unsealed jars.

Nutritional Information (1 tbsp):

Calories: 61; Total fat: 4 oz; Total carbohydrates: 14 oz; Protein: 4 oz

Vanilla Blueberry Jelly

Prep Time: 1 hour | *Makes: 6-7 11 oz jars*

Ingredients:

3 lbs blueberries

5 cups of sugar

2 tsp. citric acid

2 tsp. vanilla

How to Prepare:

1. Spoon 1 cup of the sugar over the berries and set aside for overnight.

2. Boil the blueberries over the low heat for around 30 minutes, stirring all the time. Pour in some water. Then mash the blueberries with the potato masher and strain the mixture to get 4-5 cups of the juice.

3. In a saucepan, combine the juice with the remaining sugar and vanilla and boil the juice for 30 minutes until thickened. The jelly should be thick enough to pour it into the jars. Skim the foam from the surface. 10 minutes before the jelly is ready mix in the citric acid.

4. Remove the saucepan from the heat and pour the freshly cooked jelly into the sterilized jars.

5. Turn the jars upside down or boil for around 10 minutes and then leave to cool. Check the lids by pressing them with the finger. In case some of the jars with the jelly are unsealed, place them into the fridge or reprocess the unsealed jars.

Nutritional Information (1 tbsp):

Calories: 57; Total fat: 4 oz; Total carbohydrates: 8 oz; Protein: 3 oz

Blueberry & Raspberry Jelly

Prep Time: 50 min. | Makes: 8 10 oz jars

Ingredients:

1 lbs blueberries

1 lbs raspberries

5 cups of sugar

2 tsp. citric acid

How to Prepare:

1. Spoon 1 cup of the sugar over the berries. Set aside for overnight.

2. Boil the blueberries and raspberries over the low heat for around 20 minutes, stirring all the time. Pour in some water. Then mash the blueberries and raspberries using the potato masher and strain the mixture to get 4-5 cups of the juice.

3. In a saucepan, combine the juice with the remaining sugar and boil the juice for 30 minutes until thickened. The jelly should be thick enough to pour it into the jars. Skim the foam from the surface. 10 minutes before the jelly is ready mix in the citric acid.

4. Remove the saucepan from the heat and pour the freshly cooked jelly into the sterilized jars.

5. Turn the jars upside down or boil for around 10 minutes and then leave to cool. Check the lids by pressing them with the finger. In case some of the jars with the jelly are unsealed, place them into the fridge or reprocess the unsealed jars.

Nutritional Information (1 tbsp):

Calories: 52; Total fat: 6 oz; Total carbohydrates: 9 oz; Protein: 4 oz

Apricots Taste Redcurrant Jelly

Prep Time: 50 min. | *Makes: 6-7 11 oz jars*

Ingredients:

6 cups of redcurrants, fresh

3 tbsp. pure apricots extract

5 cups of sugar

1 cup of orange juice

How to Prepare:

1. Spoon 4 tbsp. sugar over the redcurrants and set aside for few hours and then crush the berries.

2. Pour some water and boil the redcurrants over the low heat for 15-20 minutes, stirring all the time. Then strain the redcurrants to get 4 cups of the juice.

3. In a saucepan, combine the juice with the sugar and boil the juice for 30 minutes. Pour the orange juice. Mix well. The jelly should be thick enough to ladle it into the jars. Remove the foam from the surface. 10 minutes before the jelly is ready mix in the pure apricots extract.

4. Remove the saucepan from the heat and ladle the freshly cooked jelly into the sterilized jars and seal the jars.

5. Flip the jars upside down or boil for around 10 minutes and then leave to cool. Check the lids by pressing them with the finger. In case some of the jars with the redcurrant jelly are unsealed, place them into the fridge or reprocess the unsealed jars.

Nutritional Information (1 tbsp):

Calories: 56; Total fat: 3 oz; Total carbohydrates: 5 oz; Protein: 3 oz

Vanilla Raspberry Jelly

Prep Time: 1 hour│Makes: 8 10 oz jars

Ingredients:

3 lbs raspberries

5 cups of sugar

2 tsp. citric acid

3 tsp. pure vanilla extract

How to Prepare:

1. Spoon 1 cup of the sugar over the berries. Set aside for overnight.

2. Boil the raspberries over the low heat for around 30 minutes, stirring all the time. Pour in some water. Then mash the berries using the potato masher and strain the mixture to get 4-5 cups of the juice.

3. In a saucepan, combine the juice with the remaining sugar and boil the juice for 30 minutes until thickened. The jelly should be thick enough to pour it into the jars. Skim the foam from the surface. 10 minutes before the jelly is ready mix in the citric acid and pure vanilla extract.

4. Remove the saucepan from the heat and pour the freshly cooked jelly into the sterilized jars.

5. Turn the jars upside down or boil for around 10 minutes and then leave to cool. Check the lids by pressing them with the finger. In case some of the jars with the jelly are unsealed, place them into the fridge or reprocess the unsealed jars.

Nutritional Information (1 tbsp):

Calories: 58; Total fat: 6 oz; Total carbohydrates: 10 oz; Protein: 4 oz

Pineapple Taste Cherry Jelly

Prep Time: 1 hour | *Makes: 6-7 11 oz jars*

Ingredients:

2 lbs cherries, pitted

2 tbsp. pure pineapple extract

5 cups of sugar

2 tsp. citric acid

How to Prepare:

1. Spoon 1 cup of sugar over the berries and set aside for overnight.

2. Boil the berries over the low heat for around 30 minutes, stirring all the time. Then add in the pure pineapple extract and mash the berries with the potato masher. Strain the mixture to get 5 cups of the juice.

3. In a saucepan, combine the juice with the remaining sugar and boil the juice for around 30 minutes until thickened. The jelly should be thick enough to pour it into the jars. Skim the foam from the surface. 10 minutes before the jelly is ready mix in the citric acid.

4. Remove the saucepan from the heat and pour the freshly cooked jelly into the sterilized jars.

5. Turn the jars upside down or boil for around 10 minutes and then leave to cool. Check the lids by pressing them with the finger. In case some of the jars with the cherry jelly are unsealed, place them into the fridge or reprocess the unsealed jars.

Nutritional Information (1 tbsp):

Calories: 57; Total fat: 4 oz; Total carbohydrates: 8 oz; Protein: 3 oz

Blueberry Pears Jelly

Prep Time: 1 hour | Makes: 8 10 oz jars

Ingredients:

3 lb blueberries

1 lb pears, peeled and diced

5 cups of sugar

2 tsp. citric acid

How to Prepare:

1. Spoon 1 cup of the sugar over the berries and pears. Set aside for overnight.

2. Boil the blueberries and pears over the low heat for around 30 minutes, stirring all the time. Pour in some water. Then mash the blueberries and pears using the potato masher and strain the mixture to get 4-5 cups of the juice.

3. In a saucepan, combine the juice with the remaining sugar and boil the juice for 30 minutes until thickened. The jelly should be thick enough to pour it into the jars. Skim the foam from the surface. 10 minutes before the jelly is ready mix in the citric acid.

4. Remove the saucepan from the heat and pour the freshly cooked jelly into the sterilized jars.

5. Turn the jars upside down or boil for around 10 minutes and then leave to cool. Check the lids by pressing them with the finger. In case some of the jars with the jelly are unsealed, place them into the fridge or reprocess the unsealed jars.

Nutritional Information (1 tbsp):

Calories: 57; Total fat: 4 oz; Total carbohydrates: 8 oz; Protein: 3 oz

Blackberry Jelly

Prep Time: 1 hour | Makes: 8 10 oz jars

Ingredients:

3 lb blackberries

5 cups of sugar

3 tsp. citric acid

How to Prepare:

1. Spoon 1 cup of the sugar over the berries. Set aside for overnight.

2. Boil the blackberries on a low heat for around 30 minutes, stirring all the time. Pour in some water. Then mash the blackberries using the potato masher and strain the mixture to get 4-5 cups of the juice.

3. In a saucepan, combine the juice with the remaining sugar and boil the juice for 30 minutes until thickened. The jelly should be thick enough to pour it into the jars. Skim the foam from the surface. 10 minutes before the jelly is ready mix in the citric acid.

4. Remove the saucepan from the heat and pour the freshly cooked jelly into the sterilized jars or bottles.

5. Turn the jars upside down or boil for around 10 minutes and then leave to cool. Check the lids by pressing them with the finger. In case some of the jars or bottles with the blackberry jelly are unsealed, place them into the fridge or reprocess the unsealed jars.

Nutritional Information (1 tbsp):

Calories: 58; Total fat: 6 oz; Total carbohydrates: 10 oz; Protein: 4 oz

Blackberry & Strawberry Jelly

Prep Time: 1 hour | Makes: 7 12 oz jars

Ingredients:

3 lb blackberries

2 lb strawberries

5 cups of sugar

3 tsp. citric acid

How to Prepare:

1. Spoon 1 cup of the sugar over the berries. Set aside for overnight.

2. Boil the blackberries and strawberries on a low heat for around 30 minutes, stirring all the time. Pour in some water. Then mash the berries using the potato masher and strain the mixture to get 5-6 cups of juice.

3. In a saucepan, combine the juice with the remaining sugar and boil the juice for 30 minutes until thickened. The jelly should be thick enough to pour it into the jars. Skim the foam from the surface. 10 minutes before the jelly is ready mix in the citric acid.

4. Remove the saucepan from the heat and pour the freshly cooked jelly into the sterilized jars or bottles.

5. Turn the jars upside down or boil for around 10 minutes and then leave to cool. Check the lids by pressing them with the finger. In case some of the jars or bottles with the jelly are unsealed, place them into the fridge or reprocess the unsealed jars.

Nutritional Information (1 tbsp):

Calories: 67; Total fat: 8 oz; Total carbohydrates: 14 oz; Protein: 5 oz

Blackberry & Kiwi Jelly

Prep Time: 1 hour│Makes: 7 12 oz jars

Ingredients:

3 lb blackberries

2 lb kiwis, peeled and diced

2 tbsp. agar-agar

5 cups of sugar

How to Prepare:

1. Spoon 1 cup of the sugar over the blackberries.

2. Boil the blackberries on a low heat for around 30 minutes, stirring all the time. Pour in some water. Then mash the berries using the potato masher and strain the mixture to get 5-6 cups of juice.

3. In a saucepan, combine the blackberry juice, kiwis and remaining sugar. Boil the juice for 30 minutes until thickened. The jelly should be thick enough to pour it into the jars. Skim the foam from the surface. 10 minutes before the jelly is ready mix in the agar-agar.

4. Remove the saucepan from the heat and pour the freshly cooked jelly into the sterilized jars or bottles.

5. Turn the jars upside down or boil for around 10 minutes and then leave to cool. Check the lids by pressing them with the finger. In case some of the jars or bottles with the jelly are unsealed, place them into the fridge or reprocess the unsealed jars.

Nutritional Information (1 tbsp):

Calories: 62; Total fat: 9 oz; Total carbohydrates: 13 oz; Protein: 6 oz

Plum Jelly with Pineapples

Prep Time: 1 hour | Makes: 8 10 oz jars

Ingredients:

2 lbs plums, pitted

2 lbs pineapples, diced

5 cups of sugar

2 tsp. citric acid

How to Prepare:

1. Spoon 1 cup of the sugar over the plums and pineapples. Set aside for overnight.

2. Boil the plums over the low heat for around 30 minutes, stirring all the time. Pour in some water and add the pineapples. Then mash the plums using the potato masher and strain the mixture to get 4-5 cups of juice.

3. In a saucepan, combine the juice with the remaining sugar and boil the juice for 30 minutes until thickened. The jelly should be thick enough to pour it into the jars. Skim the foam from the surface. 10 minutes before the jelly is ready mix in the citric acid.

4. Remove the saucepan from the heat and pour the freshly cooked jelly into the sterilized jars.

5. Turn the jars upside down or boil for around 10 minutes and then leave to cool. Check the lids by pressing them with the finger. In case some of the jars with the jelly are unsealed, place them into the fridge or reprocess the unsealed jars.

Nutritional Information (1 tbsp):

Calories: 59; Total fat: 5 oz; Total carbohydrates: 9 oz; Protein: 4 oz

Pomegranate Jelly with Pineapples

Prep Time: 50 min. | *Makes: 10-11 12 oz jars*

Ingredients:

45 oz pomegranate juice

25 oz pineapple juice

2 tbsp. gelatin or agar-agar substitute

5 cups of sugar

2 tsp. citric acid

How to Prepare:

1. Boil the pomegranate and pineapple juice over the low heat for around 20 minutes, stirring all the time. Spoon the sugar and gelatin. Boil the juice for 30 minutes until thickened. The jelly should be thick enough to pour it into the jars. Skim the foam from the surface. 10 minutes before the jelly is ready mix in the citric acid.

2. Remove the saucepan from the heat and pour the freshly cooked jelly into the sterilized jars.

3. Turn the jars upside down or boil for around 10 minutes and then leave to cool. Check the lids by pressing them with the finger. In case some of the jars with the jelly are unsealed, place them into the fridge or reprocess the unsealed jars.

Nutritional Information (1 tbsp):

Calories: 58; Total fat: 6 oz; Total carbohydrates: 10 oz; Protein: 5 oz

Orange Jelly with Raspberries

Prep Time: 50 min. | Makes: 6 12 oz jars

Ingredients:

2 lb oranges

1 cup of raspberry syrup

2 tbsp. gelatin or agar-agar substitute

2 cups of sugar

2 tsp. citric acid

How to Prepare:

1. Squeeze the oranges. Then boil the orange juice with the raspberry syrup over the low heat for around 20 minutes, stirring all the time. Spoon the sugar and gelatin or its substitute. Boil the juice for 30 minutes until thickened. The jelly should be thick enough to pour it into the jars. Skim the foam from the surface. 10 minutes before the jelly is ready mix in the citric acid.

2. Remove the saucepan from the heat and pour the freshly cooked jelly into the sterilized jars.

3. Turn the jars upside down or boil for around 10 minutes and then leave to cool. Check the lids by pressing them with the finger. In case some of the jars with the orange jelly are unsealed, place them into the fridge or reprocess the unsealed jars.

Nutritional Information (1 tbsp):

Calories: 53; Total fat: 6 oz; Total carbohydrates: 10 oz; Protein: 4 oz

Tangerine Jelly

Prep Time: 50 min. | Makes: 7 10 oz jars

Ingredients:

20 oz tangerines

1 cup of strawberry syrup

2 tbsp. gelatin or agar-agar substitute

2 cups of sugar

How to Prepare:

1. Boil the tangerines with the strawberry syrup over the low heat for around 20 minutes, stirring all the time. Spoon the sugar and gelatin. Boil the juice for 30 minutes until thickened. The jelly should be thick enough to pour it into the jars. Skim the foam from the surface.

2. Remove the saucepan from the heat and pour the freshly cooked jelly into the sterilized jars.

3. Turn the jars upside down or boil for around 10 minutes and then leave to cool. Check the lids by pressing them with the finger. In case some of the jars with the jelly are unsealed, place them into the fridge or reprocess the unsealed jars.

Nutritional Information (1 tbsp):
Calories: 50; Total fat: 7 oz; Total carbohydrates: 11 oz; Protein: 6 oz

Pineapple Jelly with Blackberries

Prep Time: 50 min. | *Makes: 5-6 8 oz jars*

Ingredients:

25 oz pineapple juice

1 cup of blackberry syrup

2 tbsp. gelatin or agar-agar substitute

2 cups of sugar

How to Prepare:

1. Boil the pineapple juice with the blackberry syrup over the low heat for around 20 minutes, stirring all the time. Spoon the sugar and gelatin. Boil the juice for 30 minutes until thickened. The jelly should be thick enough to pour it into the jars. Skim the foam from the surface.

2. Remove the saucepan from the heat and pour the freshly cooked jelly into the sterilized jars.

3. Turn the jars upside down or boil for around 10 minutes and then leave to cool. Check the lids by pressing them with the finger. In case some of the jars with the jelly are unsealed, place them into the fridge or reprocess the unsealed jars.

Nutritional Information (1 tbsp):

Calories: 55; Total fat: 8 oz; Total carbohydrates: 9 oz; Protein: 4 oz

Plum Jelly

Prep Time: 1 hour | Makes: 6-7 11 oz jars

Ingredients:

4 lbs plums, pitted

5 cups of sugar

2 tsp. citric acid

How to Prepare:

1. Spoon 1 cup of sugar over the plums and set aside for overnight.

2. Pour some water and boil the plums over the low heat for around 30 minutes, stirring all the time. Then mash the plums with the potato masher and strain the mixture to get 4-5 cups of the juice.

3. In a saucepan, combine the juice with the remaining sugar and boil the juice for 30 minutes until thickened. The jelly should be thick enough to pour it into the jars. Skim the foam from the surface. 10 minutes before the jelly is ready mix in the citric acid.

4. Remove the saucepan from the heat and pour the freshly cooked jelly into the sterilized jars.

5. Turn the jars upside down or boil for around 10 minutes and then leave to cool. Check the lids by pressing them with the finger. In case some of the jars with the plum jelly are unsealed, place them into the fridge or reprocess the unsealed jars.

Nutritional Information (1 tbsp):

Calories: 65; Total fat: 5 oz; Total carbohydrates: 7 oz; Protein: 3 oz

Lemon Taste Raspberry Jelly

Prep Time: 50 min.│Makes: 7-8 10 oz jars

Ingredients:

25 oz raspberries, fresh

5 cups of sugar

2 medium lemons, halved and squeezed

3 tbsp. pure vanilla extract

How to Prepare:

1. Spoon 4 tbsp. sugar over the raspberries. Set aside for few hours. Then mash the raspberries using the potato masher.

2. Pour some water and boil the raspberries on a low heat for around 15-20 minutes, stirring all the time. Then strain the raspberries to get 4 cups of the juice.

3. In a saucepan, combine the juice with the sugar and pure vanilla extract. Pour the lemon juice. Boil the raspberry juice for 30 minutes. The jelly should be thick enough to pour it into the jars.

4. Remove the saucepan from the heat and ladle the freshly cooked jelly into the sterilized jars and seal the jars.

5. Flip the jars upside down or boil for around 10 minutes and then leave to cool. Check the lids by pressing them with the finger. In case some of the jars with the raspberry jelly are unsealed, place them into the fridge or reprocess the unsealed jars.

Nutritional Information (1 tbsp):

Calories: 52; Total fat: 4 oz; Total carbohydrates: 9 oz; Protein: 3 oz

Tangerine & Raspberry Jelly

Prep Time: 50 min. | Makes: 8 10 oz jars

Ingredients:

1 lbs tangerines

1 lbs raspberries

1 tbsp. gelatin

5 cups of sugar

2 tsp. citric acid

How to Prepare:

1. Spoon 1 cup of the sugar over the fruits. Set aside for overnight.

2. Boil the fruits over the low heat for around 20 minutes, stirring all the time. Pour in some water. Then mash the fruits using the potato masher and strain the mixture to get 4-5 cups of the juice.

3. In a saucepan, combine the juice with the remaining sugar and gelatin and boil the juice for 30 minutes until thickened. The jelly should be thick enough to pour it into the jars. Skim the foam from the surface. 10 minutes before the jelly is ready mix in the citric acid.

4. Remove the saucepan from the heat and pour the freshly cooked jelly into the sterilized jars.

5. Turn the jars upside down or boil for around 10 minutes and then leave to cool. Check the lids by pressing them with the finger. In case some of the jars with the jelly are unsealed, place them into the fridge or reprocess the unsealed jars.

Nutritional Information (1 tbsp):

Calories: 52; Total fat: 6 oz; Total carbohydrates: 9 oz; Protein: 4 oz

Redcurrant Jelly

Prep Time: 50 min. | *Makes: 6-7 11 oz jars*

Ingredients:

2 lbs redcurrants, fresh

1 tbsp gelatin

5 cups of sugar

How to Prepare:

1. Spoon 4 tbsp. sugar over the redcurrants and set aside for few hours and then crush the berries.

2. Pour some water and boil the redcurrants over the low heat for 15-20 minutes, stirring all the time. Then strain the redcurrants to get 4 cups of the juice.

3. In a saucepan, combine the juice with the sugar and boil the juice for 30 minutes. 10 minutes before the jelly is ready mix in the gelatin. The jelly should be thick enough to ladle it into the jars.

4. Remove the saucepan from the heat and ladle the freshly cooked jelly into the sterilized jars and seal the jars.

5. Flip the jars upside down or boil for around 10 minutes and then leave to cool. Check the lids by pressing them with the finger. In case some of the jars with the redcurrant jelly are unsealed, place them into the fridge or reprocess the unsealed jars.

Nutritional Information (1 tbsp):

Calories: 55; Total fat: 4 oz; Total carbohydrates: 5 oz; Protein: 3 oz

Plum and Blackcurrant Jelly

Prep Time: 55 min.│Makes: 7-8 12 oz jars

Ingredients:

7 cups of blackcurrants, fresh

1 lbs plums, pitted

4 cups of sugar

1 tsp. citric acid

1 tsp. vanilla

How to Prepare:

1. Spoon 4 tbsp. sugar over the blackcurrants and plums. Set aside for few hours and then mash the berries using the potatoes masher.

2. Pour some water and boil the blackcurrants and plums over low heat for 20-25 minutes, stirring all the time. Then strain the blackcurrants and plums to get 4-5 cups of the juice.

3. In a saucepan, combine the juice with the sugar and vanilla and boil the juice for 30 minutes. The jelly should be thick enough to ladle it into the jars. Remove the foam from the surface.

4. Remove the saucepan from the heat and ladle the freshly cooked jelly into the sterilized jars and seal the jars.

5. Flip the jars upside down or boil for around 10 minutes and then leave to cool. In case some of the jars with the blackcurrant jelly are unsealed, place them into the fridge or reprocess the unsealed jars.

Nutritional Information (1 tbsp):

Calories: 54; Total fat: 5 oz; Total carbohydrates: 8 oz; Protein: 4 oz

Grandma's Blackcurrant Jelly

Prep Time: 50 min.│Makes: 6-7 11 oz jars

Ingredients:

6 cups of blackcurrants, fresh

4 cups of sugar

1 tsp. citric acid

1 tsp. vanilla

How to Prepare:

1. Spoon 4 tbsp. sugar over the blackcurrants and set aside for few hours and then crush the berries.

2. Pour some water and boil the blackcurrants over low heat for 15-20 minutes, stirring all the time. Then strain the blackcurrants to get 4-5 cups of the juice.

3. In a saucepan, combine the juice with the sugar and vanilla and boil the juice for 30 minutes. The jelly should be thick enough to ladle it into the jars. Remove the foam from the surface.

4. Remove the saucepan from the heat and ladle the freshly cooked jelly into the sterilized jars and seal the jars.

5. Flip the jars upside down or boil for around 10 minutes and then leave to cool. In case some of the jars with the blackcurrant jelly are unsealed, place them into the fridge or reprocess the unsealed jars.

Nutritional Information (1 tbsp):

Calories: 55; Total fat: 1 oz; Total carbohydrates: 5 oz; Protein: 2 oz

Orange Redcurrant Jelly

Prep Time: 50 min. | Makes: 6-7 11 oz jars

Ingredients:

6 cups of redcurrants, fresh

3 tbsp. orange zest, minced

5 cups of sugar

3 tbsp. orange juice

How to Prepare:

1. Spoon 4 tbsp. sugar over the redcurrants and set aside for few hours and then crush the berries.

2. Pour some water and boil the redcurrants over low heat for 15-20 minutes, stirring all the time. Then strain the redcurrants to get 4 cups of the juice.

3. In a saucepan, combine the juice with the sugar and boil the juice for 30 minutes. The jelly should be thick enough to ladle it into the jars. Remove the foam from the surface. 10 minutes before the jelly is ready mix in the orange zest and orange juice.

4. Remove the saucepan from the heat and ladle the freshly cooked jelly into the sterilized jars and seal the jars.

5. Flip the jars upside down or boil for around 10 minutes and then leave to cool. Check the lids by pressing them with the finger. In case some of the jars with the redcurrant jelly are unsealed, place them into the fridge or reprocess the unsealed jars.

Nutritional Information (1 tbsp):

Calories: 56; Total fat: 1 oz; Total carbohydrates: 7 oz; Protein: 2 oz

Quince Redcurrant Jelly

Prep Time: 1 hour | Makes: 6-7 11 oz jars

Ingredients:

4 lb quinces, halved

2 cups of redcurrants, fresh

5 cups of sugar

1 tsp. citric acid

How to Prepare:

1. Slice the quinces and spoon 1 cup of sugar over them and set aside for overnight.

2. Pour 5 cups of water and boil the quinces with the redcurrants over low heat for 30 minutes, stirring all the time. Then strain the quince mixture to get 4-5 cups of the juice.

3. In a saucepan, combine the juice with the remaining sugar and boil the juice for 30 minutes until thickened. The jelly should be thick enough to pour it into the jars. Skim the foam from the surface. 10 minutes before the jelly is ready mix in the citric acid.

4. Remove the saucepan from the heat and pour the freshly cooked jelly into the sterilized jars.

5. Turn the jars upside down or boil for around 10 minutes and then leave to cool. Check the lids by pressing them with the finger. In case some of the jars with the redcurrant jelly are unsealed, place them into the fridge or reprocess the unsealed jars.

Nutritional Information (1 tbsp):

Calories: 57; Total fat: 2 oz; Total carbohydrates: 8 oz; Protein: 1.5 oz

Quince Jelly

Prep Time: 1 hour | Makes: 6-7 11 oz jars

Ingredients:

8 cups of quinces, halved

6 cups of sugar

1 tsp. citric acid

1 tsp. cinnamon

How to Prepare:

1. Slice the quinces and spoon 1 cup of sugar over them and set aside for overnight.

2. Heat 5 cups of water and boil the quinces over medium heat for 30 minutes, stirring all the time. Then strain the quince mixture to get 4-5 cups of the juice.

3. In a saucepan, combine the juice with the remaining sugar and boil the juice for 30 minutes until thickened. The jelly should be thick enough to pour it into the jars. Skim the foam from the surface. 10 minutes before the jelly is ready mix in the citric acid.

4. Remove the saucepan from the heat and pour the freshly cooked jelly into the sterilized jars.

5. Turn the jars upside down or boil for around 10 minutes and then leave to cool. Check the lids by pressing them with the finger. In case some of the jars with the quince jelly are unsealed, place them into the fridge or reprocess the unsealed jars.

Nutritional Information (1 tbsp):

Calories: 49; Total fat: 2 oz; Total carbohydrates: 8 oz; Protein: 1 oz

Orange Apricot Jelly

Prep Time: 50 min. | Makes around 5 10 oz jars

Ingredients:

3 lb apricots, cubed

4 cups of sugar

2 cups of orange juice

2 tbsp. orange zest, minced

2 tsp. citric acid

How to Prepare:

1. Place the apricots into a big saucepan and then boil them with the water for around 15-20 minutes. Then strain the apricots to get 4-5 cups of the juice.

2. In a saucepan, combine the apricot juice with the sugar, orange juice, orange zest, and citric acid and boil the juice for 30 minutes until the sugar dissolves. Remove the foam from the surface. Pour some jelly on the plate to check the density. Continue boiling and testing every five minutes until thickened.

3. Remove the saucepan from the heat and ladle the freshly cooked jelly into the sterilized jars and seal the jars.

4. Flip the jars upside down or boil for around 10 minutes and then leave to cool. In case some of the jars with the orange apricot jelly are unsealed, place them into the fridge or reprocess the unsealed jars.

Nutritional Information (1 tbsp):

Calories: 49; Total fat: 1 oz; Total carbohydrates: 6 oz; Protein: 1 oz

Lemon Apricot Jelly

Prep Time: 50 min. | Makes around 5 10 oz jars

Ingredients:

3 lb apricots, cubed

4 cups of sugar

1 cup of lemon juice

1 tbsp. lemon zest, minced

How to Prepare:

1. Place the apricots into a big saucepan and then boil them with the water for around 15-20 minutes. Then strain the apricots to get 4-5 cups of the juice.

2. In a saucepan, combine the apricot juice with the sugar, lemon juice, and lemon zest and boil the juice for 30 minutes until the sugar dissolves. Remove the foam from the surface. Pour some jelly on the plate to check the density. Continue boiling and testing every five minutes until thickened.

3. Remove the saucepan from the heat and ladle the freshly cooked jelly into the sterilized jars and seal the jars.

4. Flip the jars upside down or boil for around 10 minutes and then leave to cool. In case some of the jars with the lemon apricot jelly are unsealed, place them into the fridge or reprocess the unsealed jars.

Nutritional Information (1 tbsp):

Calories: 47; Total fat: 2 oz; Total carbohydrates: 7 oz; Protein: 1 oz

Vanilla Taste Blackcurrant Jelly

Prep Time: 50 min. | *Makes: 6-7 11 oz jars*

Ingredients:

6 cups of blackcurrants, fresh

5 cups of sugar

3 tbsp. pure vanilla extract

How to Prepare:

1. Spoon 4 tbsp. sugar over the blackcurrants and set aside for few hours and then mash the berries using the potato masher.

2. Pour some water and boil the blackcurrants over the low heat for around 15-20 minutes, stirring all the time. Then strain the blackcurrants to get 4 cups of the juice.

3. In a saucepan, combine the juice with the sugar and boil the juice for 30 minutes. The jelly should be thick enough to ladle it into the jars. If not, add more sugar. Remove the foam from the surface.

4. Remove the saucepan from the heat and ladle the freshly cooked jelly into the sterilized jars and seal the jars.

5. Flip the jars upside down or boil for around 10 minutes and then leave to cool. Check the lids by pressing them with the finger. In case some of the jars with the blackcurrant jelly are unsealed, place them into the fridge or reprocess the unsealed jars.

Nutritional Information (1 tbsp):

Calories: 54; Total fat: 2 oz; Total carbohydrates: 7 oz; Protein: 3 oz

Cherry Jelly

Prep Time: 1 hour | Makes: 6-7 11 oz jars

Ingredients:

2 lbs cherries, pitted

5 cups of sugar

2 tsp. citric acid

How to Prepare:

1. Spoon 1 cup of sugar over the berries and set aside for overnight.

2. Boil the berries over the low heat for around 30 minutes, stirring all the time. Then mash the berries with the potato masher and strain the mixture to get 4-5 cups of the juice.

3. In a saucepan, combine the juice with the remaining sugar and boil the juice for 30 minutes until thickened. The jelly should be thick enough to pour it into the jars. Skim the foam from the surface. 10 minutes before the jelly is ready mix in the citric acid.

4. Remove the saucepan from the heat and pour the freshly cooked jelly into the sterilized jars.

5. Turn the jars upside down or boil for around 10 minutes and then leave to cool. Check the lids by pressing them with the finger. In case some of the jars with the cherry jelly are unsealed, place them into the fridge or reprocess the unsealed jars.

Nutritional Information (1 tbsp):

Calories: 57; Total fat: 4 oz; Total carbohydrates: 8 oz; Protein: 3 oz

Blueberry Jelly

Prep Time: 1 hour | *Makes: 6-7 11 oz jars*

Ingredients:

3 lbs blueberries

5 cups of sugar

2 tsp. citric acid

How to Prepare:

1. Spoon 1 cup of the sugar over the berries and set aside for overnight.

2. Boil the blueberries over the low heat for around 30 minutes, stirring all the time. Pour in some water. Then mash the blueberries with the potato masher and strain the mixture to get 4-5 cups of the juice.

3. In a saucepan, combine the juice with the remaining sugar and boil the juice for 30 minutes until thickened. The jelly should be thick enough to pour it into the jars. Skim the foam from the surface. 10 minutes before the jelly is ready mix in the citric acid.

4. Remove the saucepan from the heat and pour the freshly cooked jelly into the sterilized jars.

5. Turn the jars upside down or boil for around 10 minutes and then leave to cool. Check the lids by pressing them with the finger. In case some of the jars with the blueberry jelly are unsealed, place them into the fridge or reprocess the unsealed jars.

Nutritional Information (1 tbsp):

Calories: 57; Total fat: 4 oz; Total carbohydrates: 8 oz; Protein: 3 oz

Blackcurrant & Redcurrant Jelly

Prep Time: 1 hour | Makes: 6-7 11 oz jars

Ingredients:

2 cups of blackcurrants

2 cups of redcurrants

5 cups of sugar

2 tsp. citric acid

How to Prepare:

1. Spoon 1 cup of sugar over the berries and set aside for overnight.

2. Pour 5 cups of water and boil the berries with the over low heat for around 30 minutes, stirring all the time. Then mash the berries with the potato masher and strain the mixture to get 4-5 cups of the juice.

3. In a saucepan, combine the juice with the remaining sugar and boil the juice for 30 minutes until thickened. The jelly should be thick enough to pour it into the jars. Skim the foam from the surface. 10 minutes before the jelly is ready mix in the citric acid.

4. Remove the saucepan from the heat and pour the freshly cooked jelly into the sterilized jars.

5. Turn the jars upside down or boil for around 10 minutes and then leave to cool. Check the lids by pressing them with the finger. In case some of the jars with the redcurrant jelly are unsealed, place them into the fridge or reprocess the unsealed jars.

Nutritional Information (1 tbsp):

Calories: 57; Total fat: 5 oz; Total carbohydrates: 10 oz; Protein: 3 oz

Orange-Redcurrant Jelly

Prep Time: 50 min.│Makes: 6-7 11 oz jars

Ingredients:

6 cups of redcurrants, fresh

3 tbsp. orange zest, minced

5 cups of sugar

3 tbsp. orange juice

How to Prepare:

1. Spoon 4 tbsp. sugar over the redcurrants and set aside for few hours and then crush the berries.

2. Pour some water and boil the redcurrants over low heat for 15-20 minutes, stirring all the time. Then strain the redcurrants to get 4 cups of the juice.

3. In a saucepan, combine the juice with the sugar and boil the juice for 30 minutes. The jelly should be thick enough to ladle it into the jars. Remove the foam from the surface. 10 minutes before the jelly is ready mix in the orange zest and orange juice.

4. Remove the saucepan from the heat and ladle the freshly cooked jelly into the sterilized jars and seal the jars.

5. Flip the jars upside down or boil for around 10 minutes and then leave to cool. Check the lids by pressing them with the finger. In case some of the jars with the redcurrant jelly are unsealed, place them into the fridge or reprocess the unsealed jars.

Nutritional Information (1 tbsp):

Calories: 56; Total fat: 3 oz; Total carbohydrates: 5 oz; Protein: 3 oz

Orange Jelly

Prep Time: 1 hour | Makes: 8 10 oz jars

Ingredients:

3 lb oranges

5 cups of sugar

2 tsp. vanilla

How to Prepare:

1. Squeeze the oranges. Spoon 1 cup of the sugar into the orange juice.

2. Boil the orange juice over the low heat for around 30 minutes, stirring all the time.

3. In a saucepan, combine the juice with the remaining sugar and boil the juice for 30 minutes until thickened. The jelly should be thick enough to pour it into the jars. Skim the foam from the surface. 10 minutes before the jelly is ready mix in the vanilla. Remove the saucepan from the heat and pour the freshly cooked jelly into the sterilized jars.

4. Turn the jars upside down or boil for around 10 minutes and then leave to cool. Check the lids by pressing them with the finger. In case some of the jars with the jelly are unsealed, place them into the fridge or reprocess the unsealed jars.

Nutritional Information (1 tbsp):
Calories: 57; Total fat: 4 oz; Total carbohydrates: 8 oz; Protein: 3 oz

Rose Petals & Cherry Jelly

Prep Time: 1 hour | *Makes: 6-7 11 oz jars*

Ingredients:

2 lbs cherries, pitted

2 cups of rose petals

5 cups of sugar

2 tsp. citric acid

How to Prepare:

1. Spoon 1 cup of the sugar over the berries and set aside for overnight. In a pan, heat the water and boil the rose petals on a low heat for about 15 minutes.

2. Boil the berries over the low heat for around 30 minutes, stirring all the time. Then mash the berries with the potato masher and strain the mixture to get 4-5 cups of the juice.

3. In a saucepan, combine the juice with the remaining sugar and rose petals. Boil the juice for 30 minutes until thickened. Pour the orange juice. The jelly should be thick enough to pour it into the jars. Skim the foam from the surface. 10 minutes before the jelly is ready mix in the citric acid.

4. Remove the saucepan from the heat and pour the freshly cooked jelly into the sterilized jars.

5. Turn the jars upside down or boil for around 10 minutes and then leave to cool. Check the lids by pressing them with the finger. In case some of the jars with the cherry jelly are unsealed, place them into the fridge or reprocess the unsealed jars.

Nutritional Information (1 tbsp):

Calories: 57; Total fat: 4 oz; Total carbohydrates: 8 oz; Protein: 3 oz

Apple Jelly with Raspberries

Prep Time: 50 min. | Makes: 7 10 oz jars

Ingredients:

5 cups of sweet apple juice

1 cup of raspberry syrup

2 tbsp. gelatin or agar-agar substitute

2 cups of sugar

How to Prepare:

1. Boil the apple juice with the raspberry syrup over the low heat for around 20 minutes, stirring all the time. Spoon the sugar and gelatin. Boil the juice for 30 minutes until thickened. The jelly should be thick enough to pour it into the jars. Skim the foam from the surface.

2. Remove the saucepan from the heat and pour the freshly cooked jelly into the sterilized jars.

3. Turn the jars upside down or boil for around 10 minutes and then leave to cool. Check the lids by pressing them with the finger. In case some of the jars with the jelly are unsealed, place them into the fridge or reprocess the unsealed jars.

Nutritional Information (1 tbsp):

Calories: 57; Total fat: 7 oz; Total carbohydrates: 10 oz; Protein: 5 oz

Pineapple Jelly with Raspberries

Prep Time: 50 min. | *Makes: 5-6 8 oz jars*

Ingredients:

25 oz pineapple juice

1 cup of raspberry syrup

2 tbsp. gelatin or agar-agar substitute

2 cups of sugar

How to Prepare:

1. Boil the pineapple juice with the raspberry syrup over the low heat for around 20 minutes, stirring all the time. Spoon the sugar and gelatin. Boil the juice for 30 minutes until thickened. The jelly should be thick enough to pour it into the jars. Skim the foam from the surface.

2. Remove the saucepan from the heat and pour the freshly cooked jelly into the sterilized jars.

3. Turn the jars upside down or boil for around 10 minutes and then leave to cool. Check the lids by pressing them with the finger. In case some of the jars with the jelly are unsealed, place them into the fridge or reprocess the unsealed jars.

Nutritional Information (1 tbsp):

Calories: 55; Total fat: 8 oz; Total carbohydrates: 9 oz; Protein: 4 oz

Rose Petal & Raspberry Jelly

Prep Time: 50 min. | Makes: 6-7 11 oz jars

Ingredients:

30 oz raspberries, fresh

5 oz fresh rose petals

5 cups of sugar

3 tbsp. pure vanilla extract

1 tbsp. citric acid or lemon juice

How to Prepare:

1. Spoon 4 tbsp. sugar over the raspberries and set aside for few hours. Then mash the berries using the potato masher.

2. In a pan, heat the water and boil the rose petals on a low heat for about 15 minutes.

3. Pour some water and boil the raspberries over the low heat for around 15-20 minutes, stirring all the time. Then strain the raspberries to get 4 cups of the juice.

4. In a saucepan, combine the juice with the sugar and rose petals. Boil the juice for 30 minutes. The jelly should be thick enough to pour it into the jars. Add the vanilla and citric acid.

5. Remove the saucepan from the heat and ladle the freshly cooked jelly into the sterilized jars and seal the jars.

6. Flip the jars upside down or boil for around 10 minutes and then leave to cool. Check the lids by pressing them with the finger. In case some of the jars with the rose petal jelly are unsealed, place them into the fridge or reprocess the unsealed jars.

Nutritional Information (1 tbsp):

Calories: 55; Total fat: 4 oz; Total carbohydrates: 10 oz; Protein: 4 oz

Oranges Jelly

Prep Time: 1 hour | Makes: 8 10 oz jars

Ingredients:

3 lb oranges, peeled and diced

5 cups of sugar

2 tsp. vanilla

How to Prepare:

1. Spoon 1 cup of the sugar over the oranges. Set aside for overnight.

2. Boil the oranges over the low heat for around 30 minutes, stirring all the time. Pour in some water. Then mash the oranges using the potato masher and strain the mixture to get 4-5 cups of the juice.

3. In a saucepan, combine the juice with the remaining sugar and boil the juice for 30 minutes until thickened. The jelly should be thick enough to pour it into the jars. Skim the foam from the surface. 10 minutes before the jelly is ready mix in the vanilla.

4. Remove the saucepan from the heat and pour the freshly cooked jelly into the sterilized jars.

5. Turn the jars upside down or boil for around 10 minutes and then leave to cool. Check the lids by pressing them with the finger. In case some of the jars with the jelly are unsealed, place them into the fridge or reprocess the unsealed jars.

Nutritional Information (1 tbsp):

Calories: 57; Total fat: 4 oz; Total carbohydrates: 8 oz; Protein: 3 oz

Blueberry Orange Jelly

Prep Time: 1 hour | Makes: 8 10 oz jars

Ingredients:

3 lbs blueberries

4 oranges, peeled and diced

5 cups of sugar

2 tsp. citric acid

How to Prepare:

1. Spoon 1 cup of the sugar over the berries and oranges. Set aside for overnight.

2. Boil the blueberries and oranges over the low heat for around 30 minutes, stirring all the time. Pour in some water. Then mash the blueberries with the potato masher and strain the mixture to get 4-5 cups of the juice.

3. In a saucepan, combine the juice with the remaining sugar and boil the juice for 30 minutes until thickened. The jelly should be thick enough to pour it into the jars. Skim the foam from the surface. 10 minutes before the jelly is ready mix in the citric acid.

4. Remove the saucepan from the heat and pour the freshly cooked jelly into the sterilized jars.

5. Turn the jars upside down or boil for around 10 minutes and then leave to cool. Check the lids by pressing them with the finger. In case some of the jars with the jelly are unsealed, place them into the fridge or reprocess the unsealed jars.

Nutritional Information (1 tbsp):

Calories: 57; Total fat: 4 oz; Total carbohydrates: 8 oz; Protein: 3 oz

Orange Cherry Jelly

Prep Time: 1 hour | Makes: 6-7 11 oz jars

Ingredients:

2 lbs cherries, pitted

2 cups of orange juice

5 cups of sugar

2 tsp. citric acid

How to Prepare:

1. Spoon 1 cup of sugar over the berries and set aside for overnight.

2. Boil the berries over the low heat for around 30 minutes, stirring all the time. Then mash the berries with the potato masher and strain the mixture to get 4-5 cups of the juice.

3. In a saucepan, combine the juice with the remaining sugar and boil the juice for 30 minutes until thickened. Pour the orange juice. The jelly should be thick enough to pour it into the jars. Skim the foam from the surface. 10 minutes before the jelly is ready mix in the citric acid.

4. Remove the saucepan from the heat and pour the freshly cooked jelly into the sterilized jars.

5. Turn the jars upside down or boil for around 10 minutes and then leave to cool. Check the lids by pressing them with the finger. In case some of the jars with the cherry jelly are unsealed, place them into the fridge or reprocess the unsealed jars.

Nutritional Information (1 tbsp):

Calories: 57; Total fat: 4 oz; Total carbohydrates: 8 oz; Protein: 3 oz

Cherry Jelly with Raspberries and Oranges

Prep Time: 1 hour | *Makes: 8 10 oz jars*

Ingredients:

2 lbs cherries, pitted

2 lbs raspberries

4 oranges, peeled and diced

5 cups of sugar

2 tsp. citric acid

How to Prepare:

1. Spoon 1 cup of the sugar over the berries and oranges. Set aside for overnight.

2. Boil the berries and oranges over the low heat for around 30 minutes, stirring all the time. Pour in some water. Then mash the berries using the potato masher and strain the mixture to get 4-5 cups of the juice.

3. In a saucepan, combine the juice with the remaining sugar and boil the juice for 30 minutes until thickened. The jelly should be thick enough to pour it into the jars. Skim the foam from the surface. 10 minutes before the jelly is ready mix in the citric acid.

4. Remove the saucepan from the heat and pour the freshly cooked jelly into the sterilized jars.

5. Turn the jars upside down or boil for around 10 minutes and then leave to cool. Check the lids by pressing them with the finger. In case some of the jars with the jelly are unsealed, place them into the fridge or reprocess the unsealed jars.

Nutritional Information (1 tbsp):

Calories: 57; Total fat: 4 oz; Total carbohydrates: 8 oz; Protein: 3 oz

Melon & Orange Jelly

Prep Time: 1 hour | Makes: 8 10 oz jars

Ingredients:

2 lb oranges, peeled and diced

1 medium melon (20 0z), peeled and diced

5 cups of sugar

2 tsp. pure vanilla extract

How to Prepare:

1. Spoon 1 cup of the sugar over the oranges. Set aside for overnight.

2. Boil the oranges over the low heat for around 30 minutes, stirring all the time. Pour in some water. Then mash the oranges the potato masher and strain the mixture to get 4-5 cups of the juice.

3. In a saucepan, combine the juice with the remaining sugar and melon. Boil the juice for 30 minutes until thickened. The jelly should be thick enough to pour it into the jars. Skim the foam from the surface. 10 minutes before the jelly is ready mix in the vanilla.

4. Remove the saucepan from the heat and pour the freshly cooked jelly into the sterilized jars.

5. Turn the jars upside down or boil for around 10 minutes and then leave to cool. Check the lids by pressing them with the finger. In case some of the jars with the jelly are unsealed, place them into the fridge or reprocess the unsealed jars.

Nutritional Information (1 tbsp):

Calories: 54; Total fat: 4 oz; Total carbohydrates: 7 oz; Protein: 3 oz

Rose Petal & Blackcurrant Jelly

Prep Time: 50 min.│*Makes: 6-7 11 oz jars*

Ingredients:

25 oz blackcurrants, fresh

5 oz fresh rose petals

5 cups of sugar

3 tbsp. pure vanilla extract

How to Prepare:

1. Spoon 4 tbsp. sugar over the blackcurrants and set aside for few hours and then mash the berries using the potato masher.

2. In a pan, heat the water and boil the rose petals on a low heat for about 15 minutes.

3. Pour some water and boil the blackcurrants over the low heat for around 15-20 minutes, stirring all the time. Then strain the blackcurrants to get 4 cups of the juice.

4. In a saucepan, combine the juice with the sugar and rose petals. Boil the juice for 30 minutes. The jelly should be thick enough to pour it into the jars.

5. Remove the saucepan from the heat and ladle the freshly cooked jelly into the sterilized jars and seal the jars.

6. Flip the jars upside down or boil for around 10 minutes and then leave to cool. Check the lids by pressing them with the finger. In case some of the jars with the rose petal and blackcurrant jelly are unsealed, place them into the fridge or reprocess the unsealed jars.

Nutritional Information (1 tbsp):

Calories: 54; Total fat: 2 oz; Total carbohydrates: 9 oz; Protein: 3 oz

Plum Jelly with Kiwi

Prep Time: 1 hour │ Makes: 6-7 11 oz jars

Ingredients:

4 lbs plums, pitted

5 kiwis, peeled and sliced

5 cups of sugar

2 tsp. citric acid

How to Prepare:

1. Spoon 1 cup of sugar over the plums and set aside for overnight.

2. Pour some water and boil the plums over the low heat for around 30 minutes, stirring all the time. Then mash the plums with the potato masher and strain the mixture to get 4-5 cups of the juice.

3. In a saucepan, combine the juice with the remaining sugar and kiwi. Boil the juice for 30 minutes until thickened. The jelly should be thick enough to pour it into the jars. Skim the foam from the surface. 10 minutes before the jelly is ready mix in the citric acid.

4. Remove the saucepan from the heat and pour the freshly cooked jelly into the sterilized jars.

5. Turn the jars upside down or boil for around 10 minutes and then leave to cool. Check the lids by pressing them with the finger. In case some of the jars with the plum jelly are unsealed, place them into the fridge or reprocess the unsealed jars.

Nutritional Information (1 tbsp):

Calories: 65; Total fat: 5 oz; Total carbohydrates: 7 oz; Protein: 3 oz

Lemon Taste Blackberry Jelly

Prep Time: 50 min. | Makes: 7-8 10 oz jars

Ingredients:

25 oz blackberries, fresh

5 cups of sugar

2 medium lemons, halved and squeezed

3 tbsp. pure vanilla extract

How to Prepare:

1. Spoon 4 tbsp. sugar over the blackberries. Set aside for few hours. Then mash the blackberries using the potato masher.

2. Pour some water and boil the blackberries on a low heat for around 15-20 minutes, stirring all the time. Then strain the blackberries to get 4 cups of the juice.

3. In a saucepan, combine the juice with the sugar and pure vanilla extract. Pour the lemon juice. Boil the blackberry juice for 30 minutes. The jelly should be thick enough to pour it into the jars.

4. Remove the saucepan from the heat and ladle the freshly cooked jelly into the sterilized jars and seal the jars.

5. Flip the jars upside down or boil for around 10 minutes and then leave to cool. Check the lids by pressing them with the finger. In case some of the jars with the blackberry jelly are unsealed, place them into the fridge or reprocess the unsealed jars.

Nutritional Information (1 tbsp):

Calories: 52; Total fat: 4 oz; Total carbohydrates: 9 oz; Protein: 3 oz

Tangerine & Pineapple Jelly

Prep Time: 50 min. | *Makes: 8 10 oz jars*

Ingredients:

1 lb tangerines

1 lb pineapple, peeled and diced

1 tbsp. gelatin

5 cups of sugar

1 cup of pineapple juice

How to Prepare:

1. Spoon the 1 cup of the sugar over the fruits. Set aside for overnight.

2. Boil the fruits over the low heat for around 20 minutes, stirring all the time. Pour in some water. Then mash the fruits using the potato masher and strain the mixture to get 4-5 cups of the juice.

3. In a saucepan, combine the juice with the remaining sugar, pineapple juice and gelatin and boil for 30 minutes until thickened. The jelly should be thick enough to pour it into the jars. Skim the foam from the surface. 10 minutes before the jelly is ready mix in the citric acid.

4. Remove the saucepan from the heat and pour the freshly cooked jelly into the sterilized jars.

5. Turn the jars upside down or boil for around 10 minutes and then leave to cool. Check the lids by pressing them with the finger. In case some of the jars with the jelly are unsealed, place them into the fridge or reprocess the unsealed jars.

Nutritional Information (1 tbsp):

Calories: 52; Total fat: 6 oz; Total carbohydrates: 9 oz; Protein: 4 oz

Blackcurrant Jelly

Prep Time: 50 min. | *Makes: 6-7 11 oz jars*

Ingredients:

25 oz blackcurrants, fresh

5 cups of sugar

3 tbsp. pure vanilla extract

How to Prepare:

1. Spoon 4 tbsp. sugar over the blackcurrants and set aside for few hours and then mash the berries using the potato masher.

2. Pour some water and boil the blackcurrants over the low heat for around 15-20 minutes, stirring all the time. Then strain the blackcurrants to get 4 cups of the juice.

3. In a saucepan, combine the juice with the sugar. Boil the juice for 30 minutes. The jelly should be thick enough to pour it into the jars.

4. Remove the saucepan from the heat and ladle the freshly cooked jelly into the sterilized jars and seal the jars.

5. Flip the jars upside down or boil for around 10 minutes and then leave to cool. Check the lids by pressing them with the finger. In case some of the jars with the blackcurrant jelly are unsealed, place them into the fridge or reprocess the unsealed jars.

Nutritional Information (1 tbsp):

Calories: 54; Total fat: 2 oz; Total carbohydrates: 9 oz; Protein: 3 oz

Peach Jelly

Prep Time: 50 min. | Makes: 7-8 10 oz jars

Ingredients:

4 lb peaches, pitted and diced

5 cups of sugar

3 tbsp. pure vanilla extract

How to Prepare:

1. Spoon 4 tbsp. sugar over the peaches and set aside for few hours and then mash the fruits using the potato masher.

2. Pour some water and boil the peaches over the low heat for around 15-20 minutes, stirring all the time. Then strain the peaches to get 5 cups of juice.

3. In a saucepan, combine the juice with the sugar. Boil the juice for 30 minutes. The jelly should be thick enough to pour it into the jars.

4. Remove the saucepan from the heat and pour the freshly cooked jelly into the sterilized jars and seal the jars.

5. Flip the jars upside down or boil for around 10 minutes and then leave to cool. Check the lids by pressing them with the finger. In case some of the jars with the peach jelly are unsealed, place them into the fridge or reprocess the unsealed jars.

Nutritional Information (1 tbsp):

Calories: 57; Total fat: 3 oz; Total carbohydrates: 11 oz; Protein: 2.5 oz

Peach Jelly with Raspberries

Prep Time: 50 min. | Makes: 6-7 11 oz jars

Ingredients:

4 lb peaches, pitted and diced

3 cups of raspberries

5 cups of sugar

3 tbsp. pure vanilla extract

How to Prepare:

1. Spoon 4 tbsp. sugar over the peaches and set aside for few hours and then mash the fruits using the potato masher.

2. Pour some water and boil the peaches over the low heat for around 15-20 minutes, stirring all the time. Then strain the peaches to get 5 cups of juice.

3. In a saucepan, combine the juice with the raspberries and remaining sugar. Boil the juice for 30 minutes. The jelly should be thick enough to pour it into the jars.

4. Remove the saucepan from the heat and pour the freshly cooked jelly into the sterilized jars and seal the jars.

5. Flip the jars upside down or boil for around 10 minutes and then leave to cool. Check the lids by pressing them with the finger. In case some of the jars with the peach jelly are unsealed, place them into the fridge or reprocess the unsealed jars.

Nutritional Information (1 tbsp):

Calories: 58; Total fat: 3 oz; Total carbohydrates: 12 oz; Protein: 3 oz

Peach Jelly with Strawberries

Prep Time: 50 min. | *Makes: 6-7 11 oz jars*

Ingredients:

4 lb peaches, pitted and diced

3 cups of strawberries

5 cups of sugar

3 tbsp. pure vanilla extract

How to Prepare:

1. Spoon 4 tbsp. sugar over the peaches and set aside for few hours and then mash the fruits using the potato masher.

2. Pour some water and boil the peaches over the low heat for around 15-20 minutes, stirring all the time. Then strain the peaches to get 5 cups of juice.

3. In a saucepan, combine the juice with the strawberries and remaining sugar. Boil the juice for 30 minutes. The jelly should be thick enough to pour it into the jars.

4. Remove the saucepan from the heat and pour the freshly cooked jelly into the sterilized jars and seal the jars.

5. Flip the jars upside down or boil for around 10 minutes and then leave to cool. Check the lids by pressing them with the finger. In case some of the jars with the peach jelly are unsealed, place them into the fridge or reprocess the unsealed jars.

Nutritional Information (1 tbsp):

Calories: 59; Total fat: 4 oz; Total carbohydrates: 12 oz; Protein: 3.5 oz

Apricot Jelly with Gooseberries

Prep Time: 50 min. | Makes: 6-7 11 oz jars

Ingredients:

5 lb apricots, pitted and diced

4 cups of gooseberries

5 cups of sugar

3 tbsp. pure vanilla extract

How to Prepare:

1. Spoon 4 tbsp. sugar over the apricots and set aside for few hours and then mash the fruits using the potato masher.

2. Pour some water and boil the apricots over the low heat for around 15-20 minutes, stirring all the time. Then strain the apricots to get 5 cups of juice.

3. In a saucepan, combine the juice with the gooseberries and remaining sugar. Boil the juice for 30 minutes. The jelly should be thick enough to pour it into the jars.

4. Remove the saucepan from the heat and pour the freshly cooked jelly into the sterilized jars and seal the jars.

5. Flip the jars upside down or boil for around 10 minutes and then leave to cool. Check the lids by pressing them with the finger. In case some of the jars with the peach jelly are unsealed, place them into the fridge or reprocess the unsealed jars.

Nutritional Information (1 tbsp):

Calories: 59; Total fat: 4 oz; Total carbohydrates: 12 oz; Protein: 3.5 oz

Raspberry Jelly with Pineapples

Prep Time: 50 min.│Makes: 7-8 12 oz jars

Ingredients:

5 lb raspberries, pitted and diced

4 cups of pineapples

5 cups of sugar

2 tbsp. pure vanilla extract

How to Prepare:

1. Spoon 4 tbsp. sugar over the raspberries and set aside for few hours and then mash the berries using the potato masher.

2. Pour some water and boil the raspberries over the low heat for around 15-20 minutes, stirring all the time. Then strain the raspberries to get 5 cups of juice.

3. In a saucepan, combine the juice with the raspberries, pineapples and remaining sugar. Boil the juice for 30 minutes. The jelly should be thick enough to pour it into the jars.

4. Remove the saucepan from the heat and pour the freshly cooked jelly into the sterilized jars and seal the jars.

5. Flip the jars upside down or boil for around 10 minutes and then leave to cool. Check the lids by pressing them with the finger. In case some of the jars with the raspberry jelly are unsealed, place them into the fridge or reprocess the unsealed jars.

Nutritional Information (1 tbsp):

Calories: 65; Total fat: 5 oz; Total carbohydrates: 13 oz; Protein: 4 oz

Orange Jelly with Pineapples

Prep Time: 50 min.│ Makes: 7-8 12 oz jars

Ingredients:

4 lb oranges, pitted and diced

2 tbsp. gelatin

4 cups of pineapples, diced

5 cups of sugar

2 tbsp. pure vanilla extract

How to Prepare:

1. Spoon some sugar over the oranges and set aside for few hours and then mash the oranges using the potato masher.

2. Pour some water and boil the oranges over the low heat for around 15-20 minutes, stirring all the time. Then strain the oranges to get 5 cups of juice.

3. In a saucepan, combine the juice with the oranges, pineapples, gelatin, vanilla extract and remaining sugar. Boil the juice for 30 minutes. The jelly should be thick enough to pour it into the jars.

4. Remove the saucepan from the heat and ladle the freshly cooked jelly into the sterilized jars and seal the jars.

5. Flip the jars upside down or boil for around 10 minutes and then leave to cool. Check the lids by pressing them with the finger. In case some of the jars with the orange jelly are unsealed, place them into the fridge or reprocess the unsealed jars.

Nutritional Information (1 tbsp):

Calories: 68; Total fat: 5 oz; Total carbohydrates: 14 oz; Protein: 4 oz

Banana Taste Tangerine Jelly

Prep Time: 50 min. | *Makes: 7 10 oz jars*

Ingredients:

2 lb tangerines

3 tbsp. pure banana extract

2 tbsp. gelatin or agar-agar substitute

2 cups of sugar

How to Prepare:

1. Boil the tangerines with the sugar over the low heat for around 20 minutes, stirring all the time. Spoon the gelatin and pure banana extract. Boil the tangerines for 30 minutes until thickened. The jelly should be thick enough to pour it into the jars. Skim the foam from the surface.

2. Remove the saucepan from the heat and pour the freshly cooked jelly into the sterilized jars.

3. Turn the jars upside down or boil for around 10 minutes and then leave to cool. Check the lids by pressing them with the finger. In case some of the jars with the jelly are unsealed, place them into the fridge or reprocess the unsealed jars.

Nutritional Information (1 tbsp):
Calories: 54; Total fat: 7 oz; Total carbohydrates: 12 oz; Protein: 6 oz

Pineapple Jelly

Prep Time: 50 min. | *Makes: 7 10 oz jars*

Ingredients:

2 lb pineapples, diced

3 tbsp. pure pineapple extract

2 tbsp. gelatin or agar-agar substitute

3 cups of sugar

How to Prepare:

1. Boil the pineapples with the sugar over the low heat for around 20 minutes, stirring all the time. Spoon the gelatin and pure pineapple extract. Boil the pineapples for 30 minutes until thickened. The jelly should be thick enough to pour it into the jars. Skim the foam from the surface.

2. Remove the saucepan from the heat and pour the freshly cooked jelly into the sterilized jars.

3. Turn the jars upside down or boil for around 10 minutes and then leave to cool. Check the lids by pressing them with the finger. In case some of the jars with the jelly are unsealed, place them into the fridge or reprocess the unsealed jars.

Nutritional Information (1 tbsp):
Calories: 58; Total fat: 6 oz; Total carbohydrates: 12 oz; Protein: 7 oz

Blackcurrant Jelly with Vanilla

Prep Time: 50 min. | Makes: 7 10 oz jars

Ingredients:

2 lb blackcurrants

1 tbsp. pure vanilla extract

2 tbsp. gelatin or agar-agar substitute

3 cups of sugar

How to Prepare:

1. Boil the blackcurrants with the sugar over the low heat for around 20 minutes, stirring all the time. Spoon the gelatin and pure vanilla extract. Boil the blackcurrants for 30 minutes until thickened. The jelly should be thick enough to pour it into the jars. Skim the foam from the surface.

2. Remove the saucepan from the heat and pour the freshly cooked jelly into the sterilized jars.

3. Turn the jars upside down or boil for around 10 minutes and then leave to cool. Check the lids by pressing them with the finger. In case some of the jars with the jelly are unsealed, place them into the fridge or reprocess the unsealed jars.

Nutritional Information (1 tbsp):
Calories: 52; Total fat: 4 oz; Total carbohydrates: 11 oz; Protein: 3 oz

Orange Jelly with Pears

Prep Time: 50 min. | Makes: 8 10 oz jars

Ingredients:

4 lb oranges, pitted and diced

2 lb pears, diced

2 tbsp. gelatin

5 cups of sugar

2 tbsp. pure vanilla extract

How to Prepare:

1. Spoon some sugar over the oranges and pears. Set aside for few hours and then mash the oranges using the potato masher.

2. Pour some water and boil the oranges over the low heat for around 15-20 minutes, stirring all the time. Then strain the oranges to get 5 cups of juice.

3. In a saucepan, combine the juice with the oranges, pears, gelatin, pure vanilla extract and remaining sugar. Boil the juice for 30 minutes. The jelly should be thick enough to pour it into the jars.

4. Remove the saucepan from the heat and ladle the freshly cooked jelly into the sterilized jars and seal the jars.

5. Flip the jars upside down or boil for around 10 minutes and then leave to cool. Check the lids by pressing them with the finger. In case some of the jars with the orange jelly are unsealed, place them into the fridge or reprocess the unsealed jars.

Nutritional Information (1 tbsp):

Calories: 69; Total fat: 5 oz; Total carbohydrates: 15 oz; Protein: 4 oz

Vanilla Pears Jelly

Prep Time: 1 hour | Makes: 6-7 11 oz jars

Ingredients:

4 lb pears, diced

4 cups of sugar

2 tsp. citric acid

2 tsp. vanilla

How to Prepare:

1. Spoon 1 cup of the sugar over the pears and set aside for overnight.

2. Boil the pears over the low heat for around 30 minutes, stirring all the time. Pour in some water. Then mash the pears with the potato masher and strain the mixture to get 4-5 cups of juice.

3. In a saucepan, combine the juice with the remaining sugar and vanilla and boil the juice for 30 minutes until thickened. The jelly should be thick enough to pour it into the jars. Skim the foam from the surface. 10 minutes before the jelly is ready mix in the citric acid.

4. Remove the saucepan from the heat and pour the freshly cooked jelly into the sterilized jars.

5. Turn the jars upside down or boil for around 10 minutes and then leave to cool. Check the lids by pressing them with the finger. In case some of the jars with the jelly are unsealed, place them into the fridge or reprocess the unsealed jars.

Nutritional Information (1 tbsp):

Calories: 59; Total fat: 5 oz; Total carbohydrates: 8 oz; Protein: 3 oz

Cherry Jelly with Apples

Prep Time: 1 hour | Makes: 6-7 11 oz jars

Ingredients:

4 lb cherries, pitted

2 cups of apples, peeled and diced

4 cups of sugar

2 tsp. citric acid

2 tsp. vanilla

How to Prepare:

1. Spoon 1 cup of the sugar over the cherries and set aside for overnight.

2. Boil the cherries over the low heat for around 30 minutes, stirring all the time. Pour in some water. Then mash the cherries with the potato masher and strain the mixture to get 4-5 cups of juice.

3. In a saucepan, combine the juice with the remaining sugar, vanilla and apples. Boil the juice for 30 minutes until thickened. The jelly should be thick enough to pour it into the jars. Skim the foam from the surface. 10 minutes before the jelly is ready mix in the citric acid.

4. Remove the saucepan from the heat and pour the freshly cooked jelly into the sterilized jars.

5. Turn the jars upside down or boil for around 10 minutes and then leave to cool. Check the lids by pressing them with the finger. In case some of the jars with the jelly are unsealed, place them into the fridge or reprocess the unsealed jars.

Nutritional Information (1 tbsp):

Calories: 58; Total fat: 5 oz; Total carbohydrates: 9 oz; Protein: 3 oz

Plum Jelly with Pears

Prep Time: 1 hour | Makes: 6-7 11 oz jars

Ingredients:

4 lb plums, pitted

2 lb pears, halved

4 cups of sugar

2 tsp. citric acid

2 tsp. vanilla

How to Prepare:

1. Spoon 1 cup of the sugar over the plums and set aside for overnight.

2. Boil the plums over the low heat for around 30 minutes, stirring all the time. Pour in some water. Then mash the plums with the potato masher and strain the mixture to get 4-5 cups of juice.

3. In a saucepan, combine the juice with the remaining sugar, pears and vanilla. Boil the juice for 30 minutes until thickened. The jelly should be thick enough to pour it into the jars. Skim the foam from the surface. 10 minutes before the jelly is ready mix in the citric acid.

4. Remove the saucepan from the heat and pour the freshly cooked jelly into the sterilized jars.

5. Turn the jars upside down or boil for around 10 minutes and then leave to cool. Check the lids by pressing them with the finger. In case some of the jars with the jelly are unsealed, place them into the fridge or reprocess the unsealed jars.

Nutritional Information (1 tbsp):

Calories: 59; Total fat: 5 oz; Total carbohydrates: 10 oz; Protein: 3 oz

Banana Taste Orange Jelly

Prep Time: 50 min. | *Makes: 7 10 oz jars*

Ingredients:

4 lb oranges

4 tbsp. pure banana extract

2 tbsp. gelatin or agar-agar substitute

2 cups of sugar

How to Prepare:

1. Boil the oranges with the sugar over the low heat for around 20 minutes, stirring all the time. Spoon the gelatin and pure banana extract. Boil the oranges for 30 minutes until thickened. The jelly should be thick enough to pour it into the jars. Skim the foam from the surface.

2. Remove the saucepan from the heat and pour the freshly cooked jelly into the sterilized jars.

3. Turn the jars upside down or boil for around 10 minutes and then leave to cool. Check the lids by pressing them with the finger. In case some of the jars with the banana taste orange jelly are unsealed, place them into the fridge or reprocess the unsealed jars.

Nutritional Information (1 tbsp):
Calories: 54; Total fat: 7 oz; Total carbohydrates: 12 oz; Protein: 6 oz

Pineapple & Pears Jelly

Prep Time: 1 hour | Makes: 7-8 10 oz jars

Ingredients:

3 lb pineapples

1 lb pears, peeled and diced

5 cups of sugar

2 tsp. citric acid

How to Prepare:

1. Spoon 1 cup of the sugar over the pineapples and pears. Set aside for overnight.

2. Boil the pineapples and pears over the low heat for around 30 minutes, stirring all the time. Pour in some water. Then mash the pineapples and pears using the potato masher and strain the mixture to get 4-5 cups of juice.

3. In a saucepan, combine the juice with the remaining sugar and boil the juice for 30 minutes until thickened. The jelly should be thick enough to pour it into the jars. Skim the foam from the surface. 10 minutes before the jelly is ready mix in the citric acid.

4. Remove the saucepan from the heat and pour the freshly cooked jelly into the sterilized jars.

5. Turn the jars upside down or boil for around 10 minutes and then leave to cool. Check the lids by pressing them with the finger. In case some of the jars with the jelly are unsealed, place them into the fridge or reprocess the unsealed jars.

Nutritional Information (1 tbsp):

Calories: 59; Total fat: 4 oz; Total carbohydrates: 10 oz; Protein: 3 oz

Pineapple & Strawberry Jelly

Prep Time: 1 hour | Makes: 7-8 11 oz jars

Ingredients:

3 lb pineapples

2 lb strawberries

2 tbsp. gelatin

5 cups of sugar

2 tsp. citric acid

How to Prepare:

1. Spoon 1 cup of sugar over the pineapples and strawberries. Set aside for overnight.

2. Boil the pineapples and strawberries over the low heat for around 30 minutes, stirring all the time. Pour in some water. Then mash the pineapples and strawberries using the potato masher and strain the mixture to get 4-5 cups of juice.

3. In a saucepan, combine the juice with the remaining sugar and gelatin and boil the juice for 30 minutes until thickened. The jelly should be thick enough to pour it into the jars. Skim the foam from the surface. 10 minutes before the jelly is ready mix in the citric acid.

4. Remove the saucepan from the heat and pour the freshly cooked jelly into the sterilized jars.

5. Turn the jars upside down or boil for around 10 minutes and then leave to cool. Check the lids by pressing them with the finger. In case some of the jars with the pineapple and strawberry jelly are unsealed, place them into the fridge or reprocess the unsealed jars.

Nutritional Information (1 tbsp):

Calories: 60; Total fat: 5 oz; Total carbohydrates: 11 oz; Protein: 3 oz

Orange Taste Gooseberry Jelly

Prep Time: 50 min. | *Makes: 6-7 11 oz jars*

Ingredients:

4 lb gooseberries

1 orange, peeled and cubed

2 tbsp. orange zest, minced

1 tbsp. gelatin

5 cups of sugar

3 tbsp. pure vanilla extract

How to Prepare:

1. Spoon 4 tbsp. sugar over the gooseberries and set aside for few hours and then mash the fruits using the potato masher.

2. Pour some water and boil the gooseberries over the low heat for around 15-20 minutes, stirring all the time. Then strain the berries to get 4-5 cups of juice.

3. In a saucepan, combine the juice with the gooseberries, oranges, orange zest, pure vanilla extract, gelatin and the remaining sugar. Boil the juice for 30 minutes. The jelly should be thick enough to pour it into the jars.

4. Remove the saucepan from the heat and pour the freshly cooked jelly into the sterilized jars and seal the jars.

5. Flip the jars upside down or boil for around 10 minutes and then leave to cool. Check the lids by pressing them with the finger. In case some of the jars with the gooseberry jelly are unsealed, place them into the fridge or reprocess the unsealed jars.

Nutritional Information (1 tbsp):

Calories: 61; Total fat: 4 oz; Total carbohydrates: 14 oz; Protein: 4 oz

Kiwi & Redcurrant Jelly

Prep Time: 1 hour | Makes: 6-7 11 oz jars

Ingredients:

2 lb redcurrants

2 lb kiwis, peeled and diced

5 cups of sugar

1 tsp. pure vanilla extract

How to Prepare:

1. Spoon 1 cup of sugar over the redcurrants and set aside for overnight.

2. Pour 5 cups of water and boil the berries with the kiwis over the low heat for around 30 minutes, stirring all the time. Then strain the redcurrants mixture to get 4-5 cups of the juice.

3. In a saucepan, combine the juice with the remaining sugar and boil the juice for 30 minutes until thickened. The jelly should be thick enough to pour it into the jars. Skim the foam from the surface. 10 minutes before the jelly is ready mix in the pure vanilla extract.

4. Remove the saucepan from the heat and pour the freshly cooked jelly into the sterilized jars.

5. Turn the jars upside down or boil for around 10 minutes and then leave to cool. Check the lids by pressing them with the finger. In case some of the jars with the redcurrant jelly are unsealed, place them into the fridge or reprocess the unsealed jars.

Nutritional Information (1 tbsp):

Calories: 62; Total fat: 4 oz; Total carbohydrates: 13 oz; Protein: 3.4 oz

Banana Taste Pomegranate Jelly

Prep Time: 50 min. | *Makes: 5-6 10 oz jars*

Ingredients:

50 oz pomegranate juice

4 tbsp. pure banana extract

2 tbsp. gelatin or agar-agar substitute

5 cups of sugar

2 tsp. citric acid

How to Prepare:

1. Boil the pomegranate juice over the low heat for around 20 minutes, stirring all the time. Spoon the sugar, pure banana extract and gelatin. Boil the juice for 30 minutes until thickened. The jelly should be thick enough to pour it into the jars. Skim the foam from the surface. 10 minutes before the jelly is ready mix in the citric acid.

2. Remove the saucepan from the heat and pour the freshly cooked jelly into the sterilized jars.

3. Turn the jars upside down or boil for around 10 minutes and then leave to cool. Check the lids by pressing them with the finger. In case some of the jars with the jelly are unsealed, place them into the fridge or reprocess the unsealed jars.

Nutritional Information (1 tbsp):

Calories: 57; Total fat: 6 oz; Total carbohydrates: 12 oz; Protein: 5 oz

Blackberry Jelly with Orange Juice

Prep Time: 1 hour│Makes: 6-7 11 oz jars

Ingredients:

5 lb blackberries

2 cups of orange juice

2 tbsp. gelatin

5 cups of sugar

2 tsp. citric acid

How to Prepare:

1. Spoon 1 cup of sugar over the blackberries and set aside for overnight.

2. Boil the blackberries over the low heat for around 30 minutes, stirring all the time. Pour in some water. Then mash the blackberries with the potato masher and strain the mixture to get 4-5 cups of the juice.

3. In a saucepan, combine the juice with the remaining sugar and boil the juice for 30 minutes until thickened. The jelly should be thick enough to pour it into the jars. Skim the foam from the surface. 10 minutes before the jelly is ready mix in the citric acid.

4. Remove the saucepan from the heat and pour the freshly cooked jelly into the sterilized jars.

5. Turn the jars upside down or boil for around 10 minutes and then leave to cool. Check the lids by pressing them with the finger. In case some of the jars with the blueberry jelly are unsealed, place them into the fridge or reprocess the unsealed jars.

Nutritional Information (1 tbsp):

Calories: 57; Total fat: 4 oz; Total carbohydrates: 8 oz; Protein: 3 oz

Lemon Taste & Blueberry Jelly

Prep Time: 50 min. | Makes: 6-7 11 oz jars

Ingredients:

4 lb blueberries

2 tbsp. lemon zest, minced

1 tbsp. gelatin

4 cups of sugar

3 tbsp. pure vanilla extract

How to Prepare:

1. Spoon 4 tbsp. sugar over the blueberries and set aside for few hours and then mash the berries using the potato masher.

2. Pour some water and boil the blueberries over the low heat for around 15-20 minutes, stirring all the time. Then strain the berries to get 4-5 cups of juice.

3. In a saucepan, combine the juice with the gelatin, lemon zest, pure vanilla extract and remaining sugar. Boil the juice for 30 minutes. The jelly should be thick enough to pour it into the jars.

4. Remove the saucepan from the heat and pour the freshly cooked jelly into the sterilized jars and seal the jars.

5. Flip the jars upside down or boil for around 10 minutes and then leave to cool. Check the lids by pressing them with the finger. In case some of the jars with the blueberry jelly are unsealed, place them into the fridge or reprocess the unsealed jars.

Nutritional Information (1 tbsp):

Calories: 61; Total fat: 4 oz; Total carbohydrates: 14 oz; Protein: 4 oz

Blackberry-Orange Jelly

Prep Time: 1 hour | Makes: 8 10 oz jars

Ingredients:

3 lb blackberries

4 tbsp. orange juice

5 cups of sugar

2 tsp. orange zest

How to Prepare:

1. Spoon 1 cup of sugar over the berries. Set aside for overnight.

2. Boil the blackberries over the low heat for around 30 minutes, stirring all the time. Pour in some water. Then mash the berries using the potato masher and strain the mixture to get 4-5 cups of juice.

3. In a saucepan, combine the juice with the remaining sugar, orange juice and orange zest. Then boil the juice for 30 minutes until thickened. The jelly should be thick enough to pour it into the jars. Skim the foam from the surface.

4. Remove the saucepan from the heat and pour the freshly cooked jelly into the sterilized jars.

5. Turn the jars upside down or boil for around 10 minutes and then leave to cool. Check the lids by pressing them with the finger. In case some of the jars with the blackberry-orange jelly are unsealed, place them into the fridge or reprocess the unsealed jars.

Nutritional Information (1 tbsp):

Calories: 55; Total fat: 4 oz; Total carbohydrates: 10 oz; Protein: 3 oz

Lemon-Vanilla Raspberry Jelly

Prep Time: 50 min. | Makes: 6-7 10 oz jars

Ingredients:

2 lb raspberry syrup

3 cups of sugar

2 tbsp. gelatin

2 tbsp. lemon zest

2 tbsp. pure vanilla extract

How to Prepare:

1. Combine the raspberry syrup with the sugar. Heat the syrup to melt the sugar.

2. Pour some water and boil the syrup on a low heat for around 15-20 minutes, stirring all the time.

3. In a saucepan, combine the syrup and pure vanilla extract. Spoon the lemon zest and gelatin. Boil the raspberry syrup for 30 minutes. The jelly should be thick enough to pour it into the jars.

4. Remove the saucepan from the heat and ladle the freshly cooked jelly into the sterilized jars and seal the jars.

5. Flip the jars upside down or boil for 10 minutes and then leave to cool. Check the lids by pressing them with the finger. In case some of the jars with the raspberry jelly are unsealed, place them into the fridge or reprocess the unsealed jars.

Nutritional Information (1 tbsp):

Calories: 51; Total fat: 2 oz; Total carbohydrates: 11 oz; Protein: 3 oz

Blackberry-Pineapple Jelly

Prep Time: 1 hour | *Makes: 8 10 oz jars*

Ingredients:

3 lb blackberries

2 lb pineapple, diced

4 tbsp. lemon juice

5 cups of sugar

2 tsp. lemon zest

How to Prepare:

1. Spoon 1 cup of sugar over the berries.

2. Boil the blackberries over the low heat for around 30 minutes, stirring all the time. Pour in some water. Then mash the berries with the potato masher and strain the mixture to get 4-5 cups of the juice.

3. In a saucepan, combine the juice with the remaining sugar, lemon juice, pineapple and lemon zest. Then boil the juice for 30 minutes until thickened. The jelly should be thick enough to pour it into the jars. Skim the foam from the surface.

4. Remove the saucepan from the heat and pour the freshly cooked jelly into the sterilized jars.

5. Turn the jars upside down or boil for around 10 minutes and then leave to cool. Check the lids by pressing them with the finger. In case some of the jars with the blackberry-pineapple jelly are unsealed, place them into the fridge or reprocess the unsealed jars.

Nutritional Information (1 tbsp):

Calories: 54; Total fat: 6 oz; Total carbohydrates: 11 oz; Protein: 4 oz

Cherry-Lemon Jelly

Prep Time: 50 min. | *Makes: 6-7 11 oz jars*

Ingredients:

6 cups of cherry, pitted

2 cups of sweet cherry syrup

5 cups of sugar

3 tbsp. lemon zest

How to Prepare:

1. Spoon 4 tbsp. sugar over the cherries and set aside for few hours and then mash the berries using the potato masher.

2. Pour some water and boil the cherries over the low heat for around 15-20 minutes, stirring all the time. Then strain the cherries to get 4 cups of juice.

3. In a saucepan, combine the juice with the cherry syrup, lemon zest and sugar and boil the juice for 30 minutes. The jelly should be thick enough to ladle it into the jars. If not, add more sugar. Remove the foam from the surface.

4. Remove the saucepan from the heat and ladle the freshly cooked jelly into the sterilized jars and seal the jars.

5. Flip the jars upside down or boil for around 10 minutes and then leave to cool. Check the lids by pressing them with the finger. In case some of the jars with the cherry jelly are unsealed, place them into the fridge or reprocess the unsealed jars.

Nutritional Information (1 tbsp):

Calories: 55; Total fat: 3 oz; Total carbohydrates: 11 oz; Protein: 2.5 oz

Orange Jelly with Tangerines

Prep Time: 40 min. | Makes: 6-7 10 oz jars

Ingredients:

6 cups of orange juice, peeled and diced

3 lb tangerines

2 tbsp. gelatin

4 cups of sugar

2 tsp. orange zest

How to Prepare:

1. Spoon 1 cup of the sugar over the oranges and set aside.

2. Squeeze the tangerines and stir in the gelatin. Boil the juice over the low heat for around 20 minutes, stirring all the time.

3. In a saucepan, combine the tangerines juice with the remaining sugar, orange zest and orange juice. Boil the juice for 20 minutes until thickened. The jelly should be thick enough to pour it into the jars. Skim the foam from the surface.

4. Remove the saucepan from the heat and pour the freshly cooked jelly into the sterilized jars.

5. Turn the jars upside down or boil for around 10 minutes and then leave to cool. Check the lids by pressing them with the finger. In case some of the jars with the jelly are unsealed, place them into the fridge or reprocess the unsealed jars.

Nutritional Information (1 tbsp):

Calories: 53; Total fat: 5 oz; Total carbohydrates: 12 oz; Protein: 4 oz

Mango Taste Blackcurrant Jelly

Prep Time: 50 min. | ***Makes: 6-7 11 oz jars***

Ingredients:

6 cups of blackcurrants, fresh

5 cups of sugar

3 tbsp. pure mango extract

How to Prepare:

1. Spoon 4 tbsp. sugar over the blackcurrants and set aside for few hours and then mash the berries using the potato masher.

2. Pour some water and boil the blackcurrants over the low heat for around 15-20 minutes, stirring all the time. Then strain the blackcurrants to get 4 cups of juice.

3. In a saucepan, combine the juice with the sugar and pure mango extract. Boil the juice for 30 minutes. The jelly should be thick enough to ladle it into the jars. If not, add more sugar. Remove the foam from the surface.

4. Remove the saucepan from the heat and ladle the freshly cooked jelly into the sterilized jars and seal the jars.

5. Flip the jars upside down or boil for around 10 minutes and then leave to cool. Check the lids by pressing them with the finger. In case some of the jars with the blackcurrant jelly are unsealed, place them into the fridge or reprocess the unsealed jars.

Nutritional Information (1 tbsp):

Calories: 54; Total fat: 2 oz; Total carbohydrates: 9 oz; Protein: 3 oz

Blackberry-Peach Jelly

Prep Time: 1 hour | Makes: 8 10 oz jars

Ingredients:

3 lb blackberries

3 lb peaches

5 cups of sugar

2 tsp. citric acid

How to Prepare:

1. Spoon 1 cup of the sugar over the berries and peaches. Set aside.

2. Boil the blackberries and peaches over the low heat for around 30 minutes, stirring all the time. Pour in some water. Then mash the berries using the potato masher and strain the mixture to get 6 cups of juice.

3. In a saucepan, combine the juice with the remaining sugar and boil for 30 minutes until thickened. The jelly should be thick enough to pour it into the jars. Skim the foam from the surface. 10 minutes before the jelly is ready mix in the citric acid.

4. Remove the saucepan from the heat and pour the freshly cooked jelly into the sterilized jars.

5. Turn the jars upside down or boil for around 10 minutes and then leave to cool. Check the lids by pressing them with the finger. In case some of the jars with the jelly are unsealed, place them into the fridge or reprocess the unsealed jars.

Nutritional Information (1 tbsp):

Calories: 53; Total fat: 5 oz; Total carbohydrates: 12 oz; Protein: 4 oz

Lemon-Vanilla Strawberry Jelly

Prep Time: 50 min. | Makes: 6-7 10 oz jars

Ingredients:

2 lb strawberry syrup

3 cups of sugar

2 tbsp. gelatin

2 tbsp. lemon zest

2 tbsp. pure vanilla extract

How to Prepare:

1. Combine the strawberry syrup with the sugar. Heat the syrup to melt the sugar.

2. Boil the syrup on a low heat for around 15-20 minutes, stirring all the time.

3. In a saucepan, combine the syrup with the pure vanilla extract. Spoon the lemon zest and gelatin. Boil the strawberry syrup for 30 minutes. The jelly should be thick enough to pour it into the jars.

4. Remove the saucepan from the heat and ladle the freshly cooked jelly into the sterilized jars and seal the jars.

5. Flip the jars upside down or boil for 10 minutes and then leave to cool. Check the lids by pressing them with the finger. In case some of the jars with the strawberry jelly are unsealed, place them into the fridge or reprocess the unsealed jars.

Nutritional Information (1 tbsp):

Calories: 54; Total fat: 2 oz; Total carbohydrates: 13 oz; Protein: 3 oz

Pineapple & Mango Taste Jelly

Prep Time: 40 min. | *Makes: 8 10 oz jars*

Ingredients:

2 lb pineapple juice

2 cups of sugar

3 tbsp. gelatin

4 tbsp. pure mango extract

How to Prepare:

1. Combine the pineapple juice with the sugar. Boil the juice on a medium heat for around 10 minutes, stirring all the time.

2. In a saucepan, combine the juice with the pure mango extract and gelatin. Boil the pineapple juice for 30 minutes. The jelly should be thick enough to pour it into the jars.

3. Remove the saucepan from the heat and ladle the freshly cooked jelly into the sterilized jars and seal the jars.

4. Flip the jars upside down or boil for 10 minutes and then leave to cool. Check the lids by pressing them with the finger. In case some of the jars with the pineapple jelly are unsealed, place them into the fridge or reprocess the unsealed jars.

Nutritional Information (1 tbsp):

Calories: 56; Total fat: 4 oz; Total carbohydrates: 13 oz; Protein: 3.5 oz

Elderberry Jelly

Prep Time: 50 min. | Makes: 6-7 10 oz jars

Ingredients:

2 lb elderberry syrup

3 cups of sugar

2 tbsp. gelatin

2 tbsp. lemon zest

2 tbsp. pure vanilla extract

How to Prepare:

1. Combine the elderberry syrup with the sugar. Boil the syrup on a low heat for around 20 minutes, stirring all the time.

2. In a saucepan, combine the syrup with the pure vanilla extract. Spoon the lemon zest and gelatin. Boil the elderberry syrup for 30 minutes. The jelly should be thick enough to pour it into the jars.

3. Remove the saucepan from the heat and ladle the freshly cooked jelly into the sterilized jars and seal the jars.

4. Flip the jars upside down or boil for 10 minutes and then leave to cool. Check the lids by pressing them with the finger. In case some of the jars with the elderberry jelly are unsealed, place them into the fridge or reprocess the unsealed jars.

Nutritional Information (1 tbsp):

Calories: 57; Total fat: 4 oz; Total carbohydrates: 12 oz; Protein: 3 oz

Elderberry-Raspberry Jelly

Prep Time: 45 min. | Makes: 6-7 10 oz jars

Ingredients:

2 lb elderberry syrup

2 lb raspberry syrup

3 cups of sugar

2 tbsp. gelatin

2 tbsp. lemon zest

2 tbsp. pure vanilla extract

How to Prepare:

1. Combine the raspberry and elderberry syrup with the sugar. Boil the syrup on a low heat for around 15 minutes, stirring all the time.

2. In a saucepan, combine the syrup with the pure vanilla extract. Spoon the lemon zest and gelatin. Boil the elderberry-raspberry syrup for 30 minutes. The jelly should be thick enough to pour it into the jars.

3. Remove the saucepan from the heat and ladle the freshly cooked jelly into the sterilized jars and seal the jars.

4. Flip the jars upside down or boil for 10 minutes and then leave to cool. Check the lids by pressing them with the finger. In case some of the jars with the elderberry and raspberry jelly are unsealed, place them into the fridge or reprocess the unsealed jars.

Nutritional Information (1 tbsp):

Calories: 56; Total fat: 4 oz; Total carbohydrates: 12 oz; Protein: 3 oz

Loganberry Jelly

Prep Time: 40 min. | Makes: 6-7 10 oz jars

Ingredients:

2 lb loganberries

3 cups of sugar

2 tbsp. gelatin

2 tbsp. lemon zest

2 tbsp. pure vanilla extract

How to Prepare:

1. Spoon the sugar over the berries and set aside.

2. Boil the loganberries over the low heat for around 20 minutes, stirring all the time. Pour in some water. Then mash the berries using the potato masher and strain the mixture to get 5-6 cups of juice.

3. In a saucepan, combine the juice with the pure vanilla extract. Spoon the lemon zest and gelatin. Boil the loganberry syrup for 20 minutes. The jelly should be thick enough to pour it into the jars.

4. Remove the saucepan from the heat and ladle the freshly cooked jelly into the sterilized jars and seal the jars.

5. Flip the jars upside down or boil for 10 minutes and then leave to cool. Check the lids by pressing them with the finger. In case some of the jars with the loganberry jelly are unsealed, place them into the fridge or reprocess the unsealed jars.

Nutritional Information (1 tbsp):

Calories: 52; Total fat: 2 oz; Total carbohydrates: 10 oz; Protein: 1.5 oz

Pineapple Taste Loganberry Jelly

Prep Time: 1 hour | Makes: 6-7 10 oz jars

Ingredients:

2 lb loganberries

4 cups of pineapple syrup

3 cups of sugar

2 tbsp. gelatin

How to Prepare:

1. Boil the loganberries over the low heat for around 20 minutes, stirring all the time. Then mash the berries using the potato masher and strain the mixture to get 5-6 cups of juice.

2. Combine the pineapple syrup with the loganberry juice and sugar. Boil the syrup mixture on a low heat for around 20 minutes, stirring all the time.

3. In a saucepan, combine the syrup with the gelatin. Boil the loganberry syrup for 20 minutes. The jelly should be thick enough to pour it into the jars.

4. Remove the saucepan from the heat and ladle the freshly cooked jelly into the sterilized jars and seal the jars.

5. Flip the jars upside down or boil for 10 minutes and then leave to cool. Check the lids by pressing them with the finger. In case some of the jars with the loganberry jelly are unsealed, place them into the fridge or reprocess the unsealed jars.

Nutritional Information (1 tbsp):

Calories: 53; Total fat: 2 oz; Total carbohydrates: 14 oz; Protein: 3 oz

Banana Taste Loganberry Jelly

Prep Time: 1 hour | Makes: 6-7 10 oz jars

Ingredients:

2 lb loganberries

5 tbsp. pure pineapple extract

3 cups of sugar

2 tbsp. gelatin

How to Prepare:

1. Boil the loganberries over the low heat for around 20 minutes, stirring all the time. Then mash the berries using the potato masher and strain the mixture to get 5-6 cups of juice.

2. Combine the pure pineapple extract with the loganberry juice and sugar. Boil the syrup mixture on a low heat for around 20 minutes, stirring all the time.

3. In a saucepan, combine the syrup with the gelatin. Boil the loganberry syrup for 20 minutes. The jelly should be thick enough to pour it into the jars.

4. Remove the saucepan from the heat and ladle the freshly cooked jelly into the sterilized jars and seal the jars.

5. Flip the jars upside down or boil for 10 minutes and then leave to cool. Check the lids by pressing them with the finger. In case some of the jars with the loganberry jelly are unsealed, place them into the fridge or reprocess the unsealed jars.

Nutritional Information (1 tbsp):

Calories: 54; Total fat: 3 oz; Total carbohydrates: 14 oz; Protein: 4 oz

Blackberry, Banana & Peach Jelly

Prep Time: 1 hour | Makes: 6-7 10 oz jars

Ingredients:

2 lb blackberries

2 lb peaches, pitted and diced

4 tbsp. pure banana extract

3 cups of sugar

2 tbsp. gelatin

How to Prepare:

1. Boil the blackberries with the sugar over the low heat for around 20 minutes, stirring all the time. Then mash the berries using the potato masher and strain the mixture to get 5-6 cups of juice.

2. Combine the pure banana extract with the blackberry juice and peaches. Boil the syrup mixture on a low heat for around 20 minutes, stirring all the time.

3. In a saucepan, combine the juice with the gelatin. Boil the blackberry syrup for 20 minutes. The jelly should be thick enough to pour it into the jars.

4. Remove the saucepan from the heat and ladle the freshly cooked jelly into the sterilized jars and seal the jars.

5. Flip the jars upside down or boil for 10 minutes and then leave to cool. Check the lids by pressing them with the finger. In case some of the jars with the blackberry jelly are unsealed, place them into the fridge or reprocess the unsealed jars.

Nutritional Information (1 tbsp):

Calories: 65; Total fat: 7 oz; Total carbohydrates: 16 oz; Protein: 6 oz

Conclusion

Thank you for buying this homemade jellies cookbook. I hope this cookbook was able to help you prepare delicious fruit jelly recipes.

Thank you again and I hope you have enjoyed this cookbook.

Printed in Great Britain
by Amazon

33552625R00064